IAL SERIES, NO. 7 DECEMBER 2, 1942

ENEMY AIR-BORNE FORCES

PREPARED BY

MILITARY INTELLIGENCE SERVICE

WAR DEPARTMENT

MILITARY INTELLIGENCE SERVICE
WAR DEPARTMENT
Washington, December 2, 1942

SPECIAL SERIES
No. 7
MIS 461

NOTICE

1. Publication of *Special Series* is for the purpose of providing officers with reasonably confirmed information from official and other reliable sources. This issue, because of its partly technical nature, has been prepared in collaboration with the Director of Intelligence Service, Army Air Forces.

2. Nondivisional units are being supplied with copies on a basis similar to the approved distribution for divisional commands, as follows:

INF DIV		CAV DIV		ARMD DIV	
Div Hq	8	Div Hq	8	Div Hq	11
Rcn Tr	2	Ord Co	2	Rcn Bn	7
Sig Co	2	Sig Tr	2	Engr Bn	7
Engr Bn	7	Rcn Sq	7	Med Bn	7
Med Bn	7	Engr Sq	7	Maint Bn	7
QM Bn	7	Med Sq	7	Sup Bn	7
Hq Inf Regt, 6 each	18	QM Sq	7	Div Tn Hq	8
Inf Bn, 7 each	63	Hq Cav Brig, 3 each	6	Armd Regt, 25 each	50
Hq Div Arty	8	Cav Regt, 20 each	80	FA Bn, 7 each	21
FA Bn, 7 each	28	Hq Div Arty	3	Inf Regt	25
	——	FA Bn, 7 each	21		——
	150		——		150
			150		

Distribution to air units is being made by the A–2 of Army Air Forces.

3. Each command should circulate available copies among its officers. Reproduction within the military service is permitted provided (1) the source is stated, (2) the classification is not changed, and (3) the information is safeguarded. Attention is invited to paragraph 10a, AR 380–5 which is quoted in part as follows: "A document * * * will be classified and * * * marked *restricted* when information contained therein is for official use only, or when its disclosure should be * * * denied the general public."

4. Suggestions for future bulletins are invited. Any correspondence relating to *Special Series* may be addressed directly to the Dissemination Group, Military Intelligence Service, War Department, Washington, D. C.

TABLE OF CONTENTS

APPENDIXES

LIST OF ILLUSTRATIONS

VIII

Section I. INTRODUCTION

1. DEFINITIONS

The air forces of a nation fly and fight in the air. Air-borne forces, transported to battle through the air, are primarily trained to fight on and for the ground. U. S. Army doctrine on the *Tactics and Technique of Air-Borne Troops* is set forth in Basic Field Manual FM 31–30, published May 20, 1942. For those unacquainted with this manual, the following official definitions may be helpful:

Air-Borne Troops—any transported by air.

Air-Landing Troops—troops carried in powered aircraft, or in gliders towed behind aircraft, who disembark after the aircraft or glider reaches the ground.

Parachute Troops—troops moved by air transport and landed by means of parachutes.

Several other definitions, as used by United States Army Air Forces, may be quoted from Army Regulations No. 95–35, of July 7, 1942:

Landing field—an area of land designated for the take-off and landing of aircraft.

Airdrome—a landing field at which military facilities for shelter, supply, and repair of aircraft have been provided.

Air base—a command which comprises the installations and facilities required by and provided for the opera-

1

tion, maintenance, repair, and supply of a specific air force.

Airport—a tract of land or water which is adapted for the landing and take-off of aircraft and which provides facilities for their shelter, supply, and repair; a place used regularly for receiving or discharging passengers or cargo by air.

2. THE HISTORY OF THE PARACHUTE

The idea of the parachute goes back several hundred years. The first record of the use of the parachute device in an air disaster was the successful escape of a Pole, Jodaki Kuparento, from a burning balloon, July 24, 1808. From the birth of the balloon, the parachute remained mainly an exhibition medium, even to within recent years.

The first parachute jump from an airplane was demonstrated by a stunt man, Grant Morton, early in 1912, at Venice, California, from Phil Parmalee's Wright. He carried the folded parachute in his arms and threw it into the air after he jumped. The first pack-type descent was made by Bert Berry, March 1, 1912, at Jefferson Barracks, Missouri, from a Benoist plàne flown by Tony Jannus. This parachute was not actually of pack type, as the parachute was stowed in a metal cone and held by break cords. The cone was tied to the front wheel skid, and a life line ran from the suspension lines inside the cone to a belt and trapeze bar, which supported Berry, who jumped from the rear axle. In the autumn of 1912, Rodman Law made many voluntary exhibition jumps with the Stevens pack, from the Wright airplane of Harry B. Brown. Charles Broadwick and Glenn Martin developed a similar type, repeatedly demonstrated by a girl, "Tiny" Broadwick, in 1913. The present Mrs. Floyd Smith made her first jump from a Martin plane with the Martin-Broadwick pack, on April 8, 1914, at 650 feet. At about the same time, "Tiny" Broadwick demonstrated the Martin-Broadwick pack to the Army's flying school at San Diego; the Chief Signal Officer, General Scriven, reported "considerable merit, warranting its development for use in our service."

The first record of parachute use in an airplane escape is the jump from a burning plane by an Austrian pilot on the Russian front in the fall of 1916, with a Heineke sack-type affair. Later, another Austrian made a forced jump from a disabled plane, and Austrian and German pilots in greater numbers began carrying such parachutes and using them for emergency escape. Both sides used parachutes in observation balloons, but no parachutes were used in airplanes by any of the Allies in World War I until after the Armistice. They had been offered to U. S. front-line aviation by our S. O. S. as early as August, 1917, but were refused by our front-line Air Force commander until after the Germans had used them successfully.

3. AIR-BORNE PIONEERING

The idea of air-borne troops was promulgated by Benjamin Franklin in 1784, shortly after observing the ascension of the Charles hydrogen balloon at Paris. He wrote: "Five thousand balloons, capable of raising two men each, could not cost more than five ships of the line; and where is the prince who can afford so to cover his country with troops for its defense, as that ten thousand men descend-

ing from the clouds might not in many places do an in-
finite deal of mischief before a force could be brought together to repel them?" Before this, even before the
invention of the balloon, Friar Joseph Galien proposed
that with such a vehicle it would be possible "to transport
a whole army and all their munitions of war from place
to place as desired." With the advent of large airplanes
prior to World War I, the possibility of their use for troop
transport was obvious.

During the first 2 years of World War I, intelligence
agents were sometimes transported by air and landed
close to special destinations behind enemy lines by the
British. The possibilities of flying troops and supplies to
points behind the enemy lines were actually planned by
America's General "Billy" Mitchell for the 1919 Campaign. The British Handley-Pages had already been developed as the possible vehicle. The fighting ended before
the bold plan could be tried out, but the proposition
continued to be considered. It should be remembered
also that in Russia during the years 1914–1917, Igor
Sikorsky built 75 great transport planes, which were used
mainly for bombing and observation but partly for transportation of personnel and matériel.

4. PROGRESS AFTER WORLD WAR I

Taking the lead in the development of the parachute,
the United States gave the world a superior type. After
the war, the Air Service continued the development of the
parachute at Wright Field until definite models were
established as standard. A few U. S. soldiers were instructed in the parachute and some desultory jumps were
made at Kelly Field about 1920–1921. Other countries,

notably the U. S. S. R., followed the American lead; and, for a time, foreign armies took the fore in air-borne development. Parachuting, as a tactical method, was first actually tried out by the Russians, who dropped their men from comparatively high altitudes with a clockwork device to open the parachutes. By 1929, newspapers and newsreels reflected the parachute-consciousness of the Soviet Army. The Germans saw the possibilities of parachuting and developed the idea of dropping men at low heights, the parachute pack being attached to the plane so that the parachute opens as the weight of the falling man pulls it out of the pack. The first military parachute troop in Germany was formed in the autumn of 1935. In 1936, 5 years before the Germans were to undertake their spectacular air invasion of Crete, Soviet maneuvers demonstrated that masses of troops could be transported by air and landed by parachute. The Italians staged mass jumps in North Africa in 1937.

In 1933 in American maneuvers in the Panama Canal Zone three batteries of 75-mm pack howitzers were flown on an emergency defensive mission, setting a major precedent for air-landing artillery. Today, as befits its tremendously expanded role as a builder of airplanes and gliders, the United States has an Air-Borne Command and is intensively training all types of air-borne troops.

5. THE TECHNIQUE OF GLIDING

The glider was the forerunner of the airplane as we know it today, since the first airplanes were practically gliders with power. The 1903 machine of the Wrights, with which was made the world's first controlled power flight, was their glider of 1902, redesigned and fitted with a 12-horsepower engine, and with radiator, shaft, chain, and propellers. The glider, launched from hilltop, tower, or balloon, by catapult, or drawn by horse, automobile, or boat, dates to about 1866 to the glider of Wenham, who experimented with a number of gliders, patented the original type of the present-day biplane, and more or less established the effect of aspect ratio [1] and other aero-dynamic principles.

Gliding, for further experiment and to some extent for sport, was continued by others. Glider clubs, which continued until World War I, were started in several cities and colleges. Orville Wright returned to Kitty Hawk, North Carolina, in 1911, and made additional experiments, in the course of which he made a free glide of 9¾ minutes, a record which was not beaten until 10 years later. The application of power to the glider naturally dampened interest in gliding, and the technique was not generally resumed until after World War I.

About 1920, gliding received a great stimulus in Germany and gliders were towed into the air from Wasserkuppe Mountain. From the simple glider, soaring planes, very lightly loaded, of great aspect ratio, were developed, and gliding and soaring were taken up in various countries. International contests were held on Wasserkuppe, in which American pilots participated, and later, up to the present, important contests have been held in this country at Elmira, New York.

Sport flying in Germany became extraordinarily popular, the German glider flying association having over 60,000 active members by 1932. Under the Paris air

---

[1] Aspect ratio is the ratio between the span (distance from wing tip to wing tip) and the mean chord (distance from leading edge to trailing edge).

agreement of 1926, withdrawing limitation on the building of German aircraft, the country built a well-developed industry by 1933. Full-time flying training began on a large-scale with Goering as Air Minister, and, in 1935, as head of the Air Force. A Government proclamation had in the meantime put the German school system at the service of aviation. The German General Staff gave its blessing to the movement to make gliding a national sport; and by the opening of World War II, Goering had 300,000 glider enthusiasts from whom he could pick potential military pilots.

At some places the Dutch attacked transport planes with field pieces and machine guns; and elsewhere, mines or trenches caused the landing aircraft to crash before air infantry could be unloaded.

The German operations in Holland taught the lesson that complete air-borne success can be attained only with complete surprise.   This was a lesson that was later to be emphasized at Crete.

8. THE CONQUEST OF FRANCE

After entering Holland and Belgium, the Germans completed their conquest of France in short order.   They made no appreciable use of parachutists or other air-borne troops, possibly because they were achieving rapid successes with their air-supported ground troops.   German mechanized spearheads frequently performed services in the French rear that might have been otherwise unobtainable except with the use of air-borne surprise.   The impression prevails that the Germans did drop a certain number of individual parachutists disguised as civilians behind the French lines, but it is difficult to verify this alleged augmentation of the Fifth Columnists, or to establish it as a matter of any military consequence.

9. AIR-BORNE ATTACK AT THE BRIDGE OVER THE CORINTH CANAL

One feature of the Balkan Campaign of 1941 was a German air-borne attack in the vicinity of Corinth, Greece.   On the morning of April 26, 1941, when the attack began, only a few Allied officers and men were defending the important bridge over the Corinth Canal, a ship canal which cuts through a narrow point of the rocky Grecian peninsula. The bridge had been prepared for demolition, but was being reserved intact so that withdrawing Allied troops might cross safely from the northern to the southern bank of the cut.

At 0700 the German Air Force began an intensive low-level bombing assault, directed mainly against British antiaircraft defenses over an area a mile in radius from either side of the bridge. This action was supplemented at 0720 by extremely heavy low-level machine-gun and cannon attack from fighter aircraft. At 0740, Ju–52 troop-carrying planes, some as low as 200 feet, appeared, and parachutes began to drop. Several hundred parachutists—the exact number is somewhat uncertain—followed by parachuted containers and unparachuted containers, were dropped over the canal area in previously selected positions in a matter of 30 minutes. To prevent aid from being sent from Nablion-Argos, 20 to 30 miles south of Corinth, German fighters prohibited movement on the Corinth road, and kept up their strafing and machine-gunning intensively after the parachutists had landed.

The defenders of the bridge fired with some effect, but it was soon evident that the parachutists were taking up stations to cover each end of the bridge and thus deny its use to the British. At this juncture a British officer succeeded in setting off the prepared charge, and the bridge was destroyed. But though the Germans were balked in their attempt to seize the bridge, the site of the crossing remained in their hands.

10. AIR-BORNE TROOPS IN THE BATTLE OF CRETE

On May 20, 1941, the German Army launched against the Island of Crete an attack on an unprecedented scale by air-borne forces, consisting of nearly 800 bombers and fighters, 500 to 650 transport planes, and 75 gliders. The RAF could give no opposition. The 37,500 British and Greek ground troops had to contend, unaided, against about 35,000 German air-borne troops, backed by over-whelming air support. The attack began with a heavy dive-bombing raid, which was closely followed by parachute landings at Malemé, at Candia (also called Heraklion), and at Retymno and Canea. At Malemé, parachute and air-landing troops, aided by the diversionary effect of those landed elsewhere, captured the airport and cleared the way for a steady stream of air-borne reinforcements from German bases in Greece. About 60 to 80 percent of the attacking parachute troops were killed, but because the British lacked any air power whatever, they were unable to check the flow of planes and gliders. German troops continued to swarm into the island, and finally the British were forced to evacuate.

a. Preparatory Phases

The preparation prior to the air-borne attack was divided into three distinct phases:

The First Phase, May 1–10: Extensive reconnaissance, primarily photographic, accompanied by light dive-bombing and machine-gunning attacks, was carried out for about 10 days.

The Second Phase, May 10–17: This was made up of daylight bombing and machine-gunning attacks on an ever-increasing scale, both in frequency and intensity.

Thrusts were made at communications, and probing attacks to locate antiaircraft, troop concentrations, and defensive positions.

The Third Phase, May 17–19: Intensified bombings were made in an effort to interrupt supplies and reinforcements, and to affect morale. Airdromes were heavily and frequently bombed and machine-gunned. German observers made daily air reconnaissance to obtain photographs, in order to study the defensive dispositions of troops and the locations of guns and slit trenches.

b. Beginning of the Actual Attack, May 20–22

As soon as the thorough reconnaissance was completed and the supply lines had been broken and resistance battered, the air-borne troops were ready to attack. At the beginning of the attack, shortly after dawn, the bombardment of the key objective area, which was Malemé airdrome, took place. This was to silence antiaircraft batteries and to prevent the use of roads leading to the airdrome.

c. Landing of Glider-Borne and Parachute Troops

Immediately following this attack, gliders were landed in the area. Directly following the gliders, transports circled the airdrome and the parachute troops were dropped in waves of about 600 each. Positions which could not be overcome by the parachutists were indicated by flares and were then attacked by dive-bombing and machine-gunning.

d. Exploitation by Air-Landing Troops, May 23–31

Even before the defenses had been thoroughly broken, troop transports were landed carrying air-infantry troops, mountain units, and auxiliaries, such as motorcycle detachments. After the key objective area was taken and strengthened, parachutists were dropped in other areas and then the troops were spread out from one area to the next in order to make contact and increase the hold. After the establishment of such areas, new objectives were attacked in the same manner and eventually contact was made between each sector.

11. OTHER USES OF GERMAN PARACHUTISTS

During the Russian campaign, German parachutists have been employed at various points as infantry units and engineers in order to obtain combat training and experience. Casualties are said to have been high. Parachutists have been used with Marshal Rommel's Afrika Korps in North Africa. Such troops are always a potential air-borne menace to an opposing force.

12. ITALIAN PARACHUTISTS IN THE OCCUPATION OF CEPHALONIA

The first instance of the combat employment of Italian parachutists occurred on April 30, 1941, during the occupation of the Island of Cephalonia. The Axis claim that the Italian parachute infantry "met all expectations from a technical and tactical standpoint" does not agree with the opinion that many of the parachutists "fell into the sea and were drowned."

13. THE JAPANESE ATTACK ON PALEMBANG, NETHERLANDS EAST INDIES

It is not believed that the Japanese have used combatant parachutists in China, though a few telegraph operators and other signal personnel may have been dropped by parachute to reestablish broken communications in the rear of Japanese advance elements. The attack which occurred on February 14, 1942, on Palembang, an oil refinery center on the Island of Sumatra, Netherlands East Indies, was the first large-scale use of Japanese parachutists. It was notable because of the relative inefficiency of the Japanese in contrast with German successes in Europe.

Knowing that there were only about 1,500 defending troops in the immediate vicinity of Palembang, the Japanese used their parachutists as an advance guard for a large river-borne invasion force. The object of the parachute attack was primarily to prevent destruction by the defenders of refineries, and secondarily to seize the airdrome for use by Japanese airpower. A third object may have been to construct and man road-blocks to impede the withdrawal of the defending ground troops.

The attack occurred in the morning, well after sun-up. The Dutch anticipated an air-borne attack, and they probably had as much as an hour's warning of its immediate approach. Sixty or seventy Japanese transport planes[2] dropped parachutists in an area some dozen miles square astride the Moesi River. The dispersion was sufficient for various groups to assemble quickly and begin their assigned tasks.

Parachutists seized one of the refineries before the Dutch had destroyed it. The group that attacked the airdrome failed to achieve its objective. The para-

---

[2] Another account gives a larger number of planes.

chutists, who were everywhere soon forced to take up the defensive, spent the day fighting off attacks. By night-fall only a single center of resistance was left. Of the total force of 700 to 800 Japanese parachutists, practically all were shot or otherwise accounted for by the determined Dutch.

Although the parachute attack was in itself a failure, the Japanese succeeded in bringing up a ground force on the following morning. Palembang, completely out-numbered, fell easily into the hands of more than 10,000 water-borne invaders.

The aftermath of the parachute attack on Palembang was a wild crop of rumors. A few days after February 15, it was understood that the Japanese parachute general had arrived at Palembang. The Dutch in Java braced themselves for possible air-borne invasion. Into Dutch Headquarters came report after report of new Japanese parachute attacks—at Medan, Sumatra, and at Plakem-baro, Java. But up to September 1942, the verified in-stances, other than Palembang, of the use of Japanese parachutists have been only two: (1) a minor landing at Menado on the northern tip of Celebes on January 11, 1942; and (2) the Japanese operation at Koepang on the Island of Timor on February 20, 1942.

14. THE JAPANESE OPERATION AT KOEPANG, ISLAND, OF TIMOR

Although the total number of parachutists used at Koepang was in excess of that used at Palembang, the in-vaders at Koepang were dropped in two groups of 300 to 500 troops on successive days and they used 20 to 25 transport planes [3] supported by bombers and fighters, in contrast to the 700 troops and 60 to 70 transport planes used in the Palembang attack.   The success of the Japanese parachutists at Koepang was partly due to the fact that at no time was there any air opposition to the bombing and machine-gunning of the escorting planes.   The parachutists performed the mission of cutting communications in support of sea-borne landings on the Island of Timor.

----

[3] Another source says 350 parachute troops were used on the two days to cut communications, 15 to 24 men to a plane.   This estimate would reduce the planes used per day to 14 to 15, maximum.

Section III. GERMAN PARACHUTE TROOPS

15. HISTORICAL NOTE

During raids on large tenement districts outside Berlin in the autumn of 1933, Nazi police officers are said to have found that they could make surprise raids better by parachute than by road vehicle. The Russians, to be sure, had already shown the way to mass parachuting. A military parachute troop, as mentioned above, was formed in Germany in the autumn of 1935. In the following year, an experimental staff at Rechlin was conducting serious experiments with parachute troops, commanded by the then Brigadier General Kurt Student. Then aged about 45, he had fought in both the German Army and the German Air Force during World War I and later had been an infantry officer in the "100,000 Army"; subsequently he had been one of the leading personalities in the creation of the new German Air Force. About 1936, from the General Goering Regiment was formed the German 1st Parachute Regiment, which had its headquarters at Stendal, 60 miles west of Berlin. By 1939 the three battalions of this regiment were expanded into regiments and along with the 7th Signal Battalion became the component elements of the 7th Air-Borne Division, called the 7th Air Division by the British. Serving as the divisional commander, Brigadier General Student was promoted to be Major General early in 1940, the year that the Division's regiments and

18

battalions, operating individually rather than collectively, saw service in Holland, Belgium, and Norway. In Crete, the 7th Air-Borne Division operated as the main element of the XIth Air-Borne Corps, and by the end of May 1940 Student was a Lieutenant General.

16. ORGANIZATION OF THE PARACHUTE REGIMENT

The regiment is the normal unit for the tactical employment of German parachute troops. Each regiment is divided into three battalions, and each battalion into three rifle or light companies and one heavy weapons company (machine-gun and mortar company). Special armament, consisting of 75-mm infantry guns and 37-mm antitank guns, is provided in the regiment for two special companies which by analogy with American nomenclature may be called the cannon company and the antitank company. The organization of the German parachute regiment is said to have been mainly determined by the carrying capacity of the JU–52, the airplane ordinarily used in transporting parachute troops. The men are usually moved by units, a platoon of 36 men being transported in a flight (*Kette*) of 3 planes.

17. ORGANIZATION CHARTS

Figures 1, 2, and 3 show what is believed to be the approximate organization, strength, and armament of the German parachute rifle regiment, rifle company, and heavy weapons company, respectively. Variations, of course, are to be expected.

18. TRAINING OF GERMAN PARACHUTISTS

German parachutists (*Fallschirmjaeger*) are members of the Air Force who have met high physical requirements and have completed a rigorous course in one of the several large jumping schools, which are under the command of Brigadier General Ramcke. Jumping School No. 1, at Stendal, is said to have closed in December 1940; No. 2, at Wittstock, 55 miles northwest of Berlin, still exists;

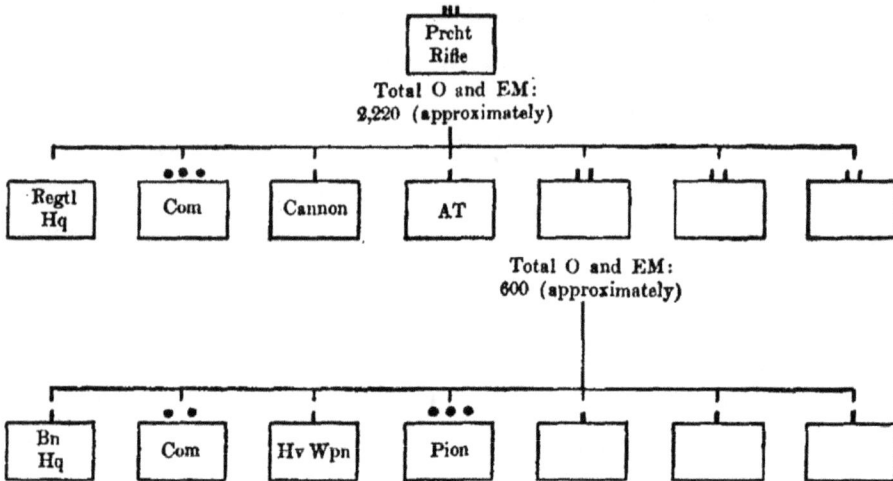

Figure 1.—Organization of the German parachute rifle regiment

Main Armament for Regimental Cannon Company: 75-mm mountain guns or 75-mm light infantry guns

Main Armament for Regimental Antitank Company: 37-mm AT guns, or more probably new AT "rifles," model 41

Main Armament for Each Battalion:

Light machine guns	32
Light mortars (50-mm)	9
AT rifles (cal 31)	9
Heavy mortars (81-mm)	4
Heavy machine guns	8

No. 3, at Braunschweig, 120 miles west of Berlin is said to have closed about March 1942; what is called Maubeuge Jumping School opened about January 1942 in the neighborhood of Paris, France. Each active school is said to graduate between 1,000 and 1,500 trainees a month, who then normally return to their original units. Parachute school graduates, especially selected for toughness, are given further specialized training in assault tactics and assigned to assault or parachute regiments. In the spring of 1941, great attention was suddenly

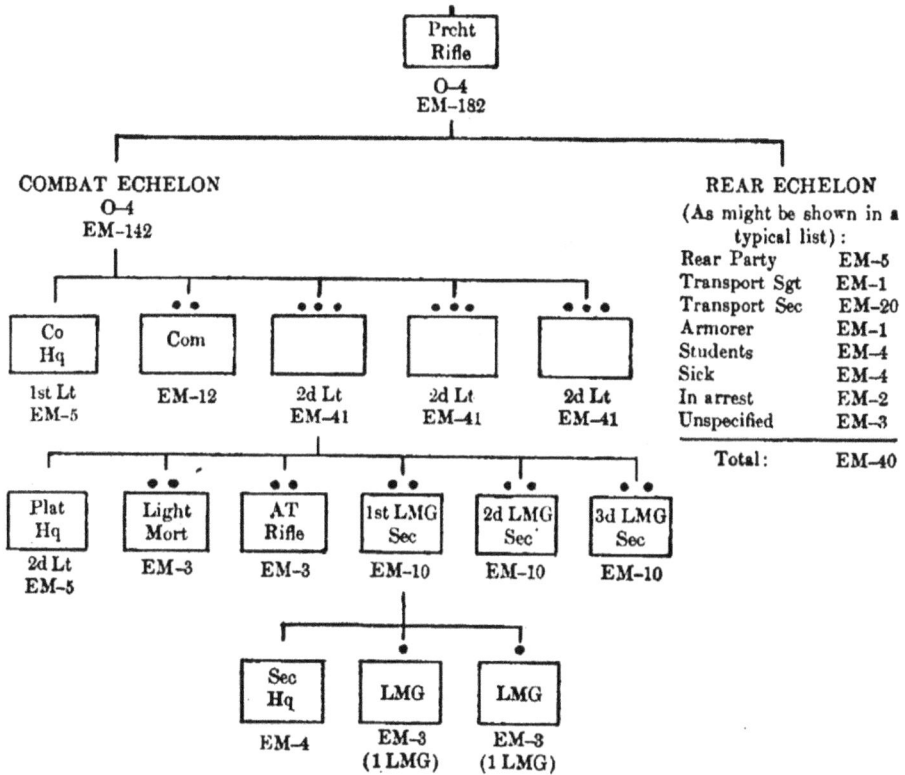

```
                        ┌──────┐
                        │ Prcht│
                        │ Rifle│
                        └──────┘
                          O-4
                         EM-182
```

COMBAT ECHELON
O-4
EM-142

Co Hq	Com	2d Lt EM-41	2d Lt EM-41	2d Lt EM-41

1st Lt EM-5 · EM-12

Plat Hq	Light Mort	AT Rifle	1st LMG Sec	2d LMG Sec	3d LMG Sec

2d Lt EM-5 · EM-3 · EM-3 · EM-10 · EM-10 · EM-10

Sec Hq	LMG	LMG

EM-4 · EM-3 (1 LMG) · EM-3 (1 LMG)

REAR ECHELON
(As might be shown in a typical list):

Rear Party	EM-5
Transport Sgt	EM-1
Transport Sec	EM-20
Armorer	EM-1
Students	EM-4
Sick	EM-4
In arrest	EM-2
Unspecified	EM-3
Total:	EM-40

Probable Armament:

Light machine guns	24
Light mortars (50-mm)	3
AT rifles (cal 31)	3
Heavy mortars (81-mm)	—
Heavy machine guns	—
Pocket knives	—
Automatic pistols (*Pistole 08*)	—
Carbines (for each man who does not fire a crew-served weapon)	—
Hand grenades	—

Figure 2.—Organization of the German parachute rifle company

```
                        ┌─────────┐
                        │ "Prcht  │
                        │ Hv Wpn  │
                        └─────────┘
                            O-4
                          EM-182
```

COMBAT ECHELON
O-4
EM-116

REAR ECHELON
Rear Party   EM-14
Motor Transport
    Section   EM-52
        Total: EM-66

Co Hq	Com	1st MG	2d MG	Hv Mort
O-1		O-1	O-1	O-1
EM-5	EM-12	EM-30	EM-30	EM-39

Plat Hq	1st MG	2d MG	Plat Hq	1st Hv Mort	2d Hv Mort
O-1			O-1		
EM-6	EM-12	EM-12	EM-3	EM-18	EM-18

1st MG	2d MG	Sec Hq	1st Hv Mort	2d Hv Mort
EM-6	EM-6	EM-4	EM-7	EM-7

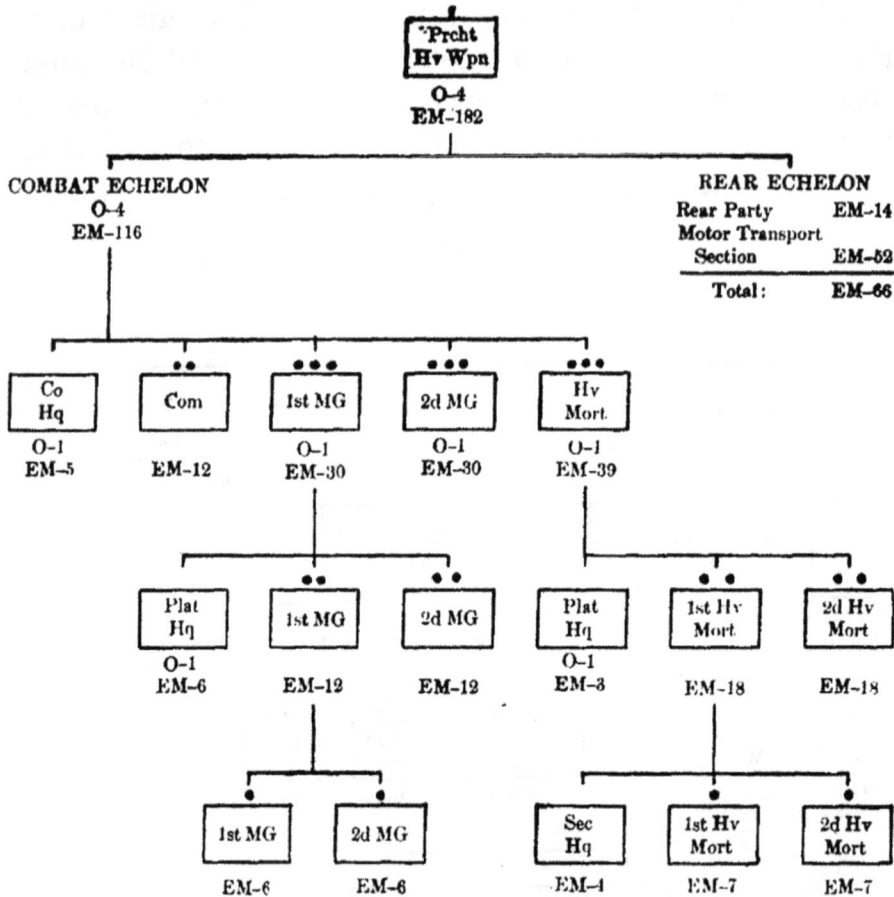

Differing considerably from the arrangement shown in this diagram, the composition of the German 12th Company, 5th Parachute Regiment, about June 1942 was reported to be as follows:

Company commander:
    1 1st Lt

Company headquarters:
    1 master sergeant (in command)
    8 runners   10 engineers
    7 AT riflemen

Three identical platoons, each platoon consisting of:
    1 Headquarters (1 platoon leader, 3 runners, and 3 LMG gunners)
    1 Section armed with 1 LMG (1 section leader, 1 2d-in-Comd, 10 men)
    1 Section (of similar strength and armament to the foregoing)
    1 Section armed with 1 Hv Mort (1 section leader, 1 2d-in-Comd, 10 men)

Figure 3.—Organization of the German parachute heavy weapons company

placed on an immediate increase in parachute troops. Numerous officers, who had seen action on the Western Front, reported to advanced instructors' schools. Training was given both in open and rugged or mountainous country, and in dropping of equipment and supplies in flights both day and night. It is estimated that more than 50,000 soldiers of the German Army now wear the diving-eagle badge of the trained parachute trooper. In each parachutist is instilled a high *esprit de corps;* he is taught that parachute troops perform a very important function.[1]

a. Progressive Training Program

The training program is divided into ground and air phases. Recruits begin their course by learning to fall on the ground without injuring themselves. Next they learn to use the parachute harness in practice jumps at a low height from the doors of dummy airplanes. Then they are taught how to control their parachutes in the air by being suspended in their harnesses from a pulley-operated training arrangement. They are also taught to disengage themselves quickly from the parachutes as soon as they have landed. Very definite details about the training of one of the men of the German 5th Parachute Regiment are given in Appendix A.

b. Care and Packing of Parachutes

One of the most important features of the ground phase is the course in the care and packing of parachutes. Each

[1] See "The Parachutists 'Ten Commandments,' " in *Intelligence Bulletin*, No. 1, MIS, Sept. 1942, pp. 19–20; also "German Officer Candidates School," in *Special Series*, No. 3, MIS, Sept. 17, 1942, pp. 47–51. "Parachute Training in the German Army" is the subject of a U. S. training film, TF 7–151, released in 1941.

trooper is made personally responsible for his own equipment, and no man jumps unless in a parachute packed by himself. (In this, as in many other aspects of their training, the Germans are not ahead of U. S. practice.)

c. Jumping Requirements

Having mastered the ground instructions, the pupil begins the air phase. This consists of 6 jumps, the first of which he makes alone from an altitude of about 600 feet. His next 2 jumps are made in company with 4 or 5 other trainees from an altitude of 450 feet. The fourth jump is made from this same altitude with about 10 other students, either at dawn or sunset in order to experience the light conditions of an actual attack. The fifth jump is made in combat teams of 10, each team being carried in one of 3 aircraft flying in formation. The sixth and final jump is made under simulated combat conditions from 9 aircraft flying in formation at altitudes slightly below 400 feet.

d. Training for Ground Combat

German parachutists receive thorough ground combat training. Their individual instruction includes such subjects as marksmanship, scouting, and mechanical training on weapons. Their unit training emphasizes combat problems, demolition work, and strenuous field exercises. The training of German parachutists for ground combat resembles in many respects that given by the British to their commando units. Parachute units, of course, must practice extensively with air units, and occasionally with air-landing units.

e. Possibility of Special Sabotage Training

The captured documents relating to the attack against Crete do not indicate that German air-borne troops were expected to commit sabotage in the true sense of the word. Damage was to be inflicted, but prisoners maintained that they had not been trained to wear, and would not wear, foreign uniforms. It has been pointed out, however, that there may well be a separate German organization for the dropping of small parties of parachute troops, possibly speaking foreign languages and wearing foreign uniforms, to create confusion, conduct sabotage, and contact fifth columnists. If so, these "parachutists" should be distinguished from the parachute regiments, which are used for large-scale open attack on important military positions.

19. UNIFORM AND EQUIPMENT OF GERMAN PARACHUTE TROOPS

The parachute rifleman, as a member of the German Air Force possesses an ordinary German Air Force uniform. This uniform has yellow collar patches (except possibly in the case of some specialists) and the name of the regiment embroidered on the cuff, but this is taken off before the soldier leaves the home station of the regiment. In action only the jacket of this uniform is worn, though the garrison (overseas) cap is also taken. The remainder of the combat uniform is peculiar to parachute troops.

a. Trousers

These are like skiing trousers, quite long and loose, and gray in color. They have buttoned pockets on the sides

495191°—42——3

of the thighs, in which such articles as garrison (**overseas**) caps and swastika flags are kept.

b. Helmet

This is round in shape, and is thickly padded with rubber, with a narrow brim and practically no neck-shield. It is varnished a matt blue-gray, or mottled, color, and bears ordinary German Air Force insignia. The strap forks below the ear, and is attached to the helmet at four points. The helmet is commonly worn with a cloth cover, frequently with a light-colored cross on top (the purpose of which is unknown) and with a band round it for insertion of camouflage; the band may be colored for purposes of recognition.

c. Coveralls

This garment is of waterproof gabardine, loose fitting and fastened by a zipper fastener up the front. The color is normally olive green (or gray-green), now usually mottled. The legs are cut short some distance above the knee; the sleeves are long and button at the wrist. On both sleeves are worn large-size "wings" as stripes of rank; on the right breast is the German Air Force flying eagle (*Hoheitszeichen*). There are two very capacious pockets on the thighs, two more on the chest, and slits at each hip; pockets are closed by zipper fasteners. The coveralls are worn over uniform and equipment for the jump; on landing, the garment is taken off and usually put on again under the equipment.

d. Gloves

These are of padded leather, with long gauntlets which grip by means of elastic; sometimes woolen gloves are substituted. They are worn only for the jump.

e. Boots

These are of heavy leather, and have thick rubber soles with a V-pattern tread. They are laced up the side, and there is a seam up the front. They extend some way above the ankle, and the trousers are tucked into them; the tops fit tightly.

f. Knee Protectors

These are of rubber, in thick horizontal bars, rather like those which some U. S. basketball players wear. They are strapped on over the trouser knee, and are discarded after the jump.

g. Ankle Bandages

These are of linen, and are bound around instep and ankle, and about one-third of the way up the leg. The heel is left free, and the bandages are not removed after the jump.,

h. Gas Mask

Of normal type, this is carried in a special canvas container. The new gas mask (*Gasmaske 40*) is made of pure and very strong rubber. An antigas cape of oilcloth is also taken.

i. Identifications

The parachutist's badge, worn low on the left breast, is a diving eagle, golden-colored, in a wreath of oak and bay of oxidized silver color; the eagle holds a swastika in its claws. (The German Army parachutist's badge is slightly different.) This badge is not worn except at home stations. An identity disc is carried; but pay-books (*Soldbücher*) are handed in on leaving home stations, and a camouflaged identity card (*Tarnausweis* or *Feindflugausweis*) is taken instead.

j. Parachutes

Types RZ16, RZ1, or 36DS28 are known. Type RZ16—*Rückenfallschirm Zwangsauslösung* 16 (back-pack, compulsion-opening parachute, type 16)—since the beginning of 1941 has been replacing the RZ1, which opens sometimes with a dangerous jerk. The RZ16, because of its ingenious construction, opens without shock, and its opening is said to be 100 percent sure. The parachutes used in jumping schools are pure silk and are valued at 1,000 marks apiece; but the combat parachutes, intended for use only once, are made of artificial silk, or "macoo." The suspension lines are drawn together a few feet above the belt of the parachutist's harness, to the back of which they are attached by two hemp harness cords; in the air, the man seems to dangle from a single string. With the airplane traveling at 80 to 100 miles per hour, the standard height of drop is just under 400 feet. After a clear drop of about 80 feet, the parachute takes over and the subsequent rate of descent is 16 to 17 feet per second (11 miles per hour). Reports on colored parachutes are various—black, white or beige, brown, and green are all used; the principal purpose seems to be ease of recognition, though there may be some small camouflage effect against the ground (but not against the sky). A more technical description of the German parachute is given below in Appendix C.

k. Individual Weapons

The combat pistol (*Kampfpistole*) is a kind of 25-mm (about 1-inch caliber) Very pistol (*Leuchtspistole*), but the barrel is rifled. Besides a signal cartridge, a special cartridge can be fired containing as projectile a light metal cylinder filled with scrap iron mixed with an inflammable, corrosive substance. The weapon has a strong recoil, and for that reason must be fired with both hands. The best range is about 55 yards, and bursts from the exploding projectile cover a radius of about 20 yards.

The automatic pistol 40 is a 35-caliber (9-mm) weapon with a length of about 20 inches. The sights, fixed at 110 yards, are adjustable to twice that distance. The 32-cartridge magazine functions poorly if filled with more than 24 cartridges. A good marksman can effectively fire in practice only about 4 charges of 24 cartridges per minute, though the pistol is said to have a decidedly higher rate of theoretical fire.

For the jump, the parachutist formerly carried only a large jackknife and an automatic pistol (*Pistole 08*) with two magazines. Men in the first platoons to land, however, might carry up to four hand grenades, and about one man in four of them a machine carbine. Since the end of March 1942, German parachutists have been required to jump with this latter weapon. Other weapons come down in weapon containers attached to "load parachutes." Experiments are being encouraged in which the individual is dropped with what he is normally equipped when operating in his combat section.

l. Rations

Rations taken, including those in the arms containers, may last German parachutists for 2 or even 3 days. Further supplies are dropped in "provisions bombs," which are described below. Special foods taken include

Wittler bread, sliced and wrapped, which is supposed to last indefinitely until unwrapped (but, in fact, does not); chocolate mixed with kola (*Schokokola*), and with caffeine (*Kobona*), which is not believed to be any better than ordinary chocolate; and simple refreshing foods like grape sugar.   Most of the food is quite ordinary.

m. Drugs and First-Aid Supplies

Parachute troops are not doped.   But the following "drugs" are used: (1) energen or dextro-energen, in white tablets, a dextrose or glucose preparation, to produce energy; (2) pervitin, a drug allied to benzedrine, to produce wakefulness and alertness.   Pervitin is said to create thirstiness.

The parachutist usually carries one large and two small field dressings.   Each platoon has a noncommissioned officer as its medical aid man.   The first-aid kit, with which he probably jumps, contains bandages, dressings, adhesive tape, safety pins, soap, ointments, iodine, antiseptics, and analgesics.   Containers dropped by separate parachute have sometimes been found to hold small suitcases of extra medical supplies and surgical instruments. Each combat company has a stretcher.   Since the rate of casualties may be high, the XIth Air-Borne Corps has four medical companies, one of which is probably an airlanding field hospital company.   Ju–52's, which will carry eight lying casualties, may be utilized to evacuate the severely wounded to Germany.

n. Arms Containers

Such equipment as the parachutists do not carry in the jump may be dropped in containers.   Four standard arms containers are carried in each Ju–52.   Each container weighs 50 to 60 pounds empty and takes a load of up to 260 pounds. Three different models have been identified: (1) a cylindrical container 5 feet long and 16 to 18 inches in diameter, hinged along its length so that it can be opened in half; (2) a container of the same length but of square cross-section, 16 inches by 16 inches, with beveled edges and hinged along its length so that one long side opens as a lid; (3) a container similar to the preceding but hinged along one long edge so that it opens in half like a trombone case. This is probably an improved design. All three of these containers are dropped in a similar manner. They are painted in various bright colors, with rings and other markings denoting the unit for which intended. Some containers have been described as fibre trunks 6 by 1½ by 1½ feet. Further details are given below in Appendix D.

o. Contents of Arms Containers

Heavy mortars, weighing 125 pounds, and other equipment of the heavy weapons company would undoubtedly go into arms containers. Explosives of all kinds are taken, including AT and antipersonnel mines. Radio equipment goes into containers that are specially padded. Among miscellaneous articles that have been dropped by the container method have been antigas protective clothing, and particularly tools and spare parts, such as spark plugs, useful in operating commandeered motor vehicles.

p. "Provisions Bombs" (Versorgungsbomben)

These are carried in bomb racks and released like ordinary bombs, which they resemble in shape. Any bomber aircraft may be expected to drop them on positions where troops have been landed some time previously. The "bomb" is about 6 feet in length and 1½ feet in diameter, having a separate compartment at the end to contain the parachute. On release of the "bomb," this end cap is torn off and the parachute is pulled out. There is no shock absorber. On suitable ground and from a low altitude, "provisions bombs" may be dropped without parachutes. Even ordinary sacks of provisions are so dropped.

q. Heavy Equipment Dropped by Parachute

Much heavy parachute-borne equipment may be thrown out the door of the Ju–52, with or without a special container. Bicycles, stretchers, small flame-throwers, mines, large mortars, light artillery pieces, and perhaps motorcycles may be dropped. The 28/20-mm AT gun, model 41,[2] has been dropped complete and ready for action, on wheels, in a container. There is no reason why a number of other weapons could not similarly be dropped complete. In most cases they are suitable for separation into several loads, but vital time may be saved by dropping them complete. The use of several parachutes together, common in the past, has sometimes proved unsatisfactory; large parachutes are therefore being made which will take loads up to 500 pounds.

---

[2] This weapon, employing the Guerlich, or "squeeze" principle, is 28 mm at the breech and 20 mm at the muzzle.

Section IV. GERMAN GLIDER-BORNE DEVELOPMENTS

20. THE COMBAT EMPLOYMENT OF GLIDER-BORNE TROOPS

In warfare the advantage of the glider over the airplane is its more silent arrival at an objective. Using the DFS 230 Glider, the Germans landed a few glider-borne troops at the Albert Canal and Fort Eben Emael in 1940. Such troops were previously in readiness during the invasion of Norway, but whether they were actually flown to combat in Norway is debatable. After Belgium fell, the Germans pushed their glider-training program. In January 1941 the partly glider-borne unit, 1st Assault Regiment (*Sturmregiment 1*), was created; and the corresponding towing unit of Ju–52's, the 1st Air-Landing Group (*Luftlandegeschwader 1*), was probably created about the same time. Both of these organizations saw service at Corinth and in Crete. The father of German military glider training is said to have been Brigadier General Ramcke, who in mid-1942 was still a leading figure in German air-borne development.

21. THE 1ST ASSAULT REGIMENT

The 1st Assault Regiment seems to have been an experimental unit, designed to be the spearhead of an air-borne attack. Although the assault regiment (fig. 4) constituted somewhat like an ordinary parachute regiment, it has not only graduate parachutists but also

glider pilots among its personnel. In Crete only two
of its companies landed near Allied troops, both being
in gliders; but the remainder of the regiment was probably at least in part landed in Ju–52's, or even dropped
by parachute (though not from gliders). It is believed
that only about 50 gliders may have been used. Each
glider carried a single combat group with all its armament. In theory the sections of the regiment transported by gliders could immediately make ready their
arms and large quantities of ammunition and explosives,
and could on account of this facility pass to serious
attack in very little time. Although all the men carried
by glider were graduate parachutists, only the glider pilot
carried a parachute. Fatalities were high because a number of gliders were hit by AA fire and fell in flames. The
supposition that the 1st Assault Regiment was an experimental regiment is borne out by the fact that Brigadier
General Ramcke took command during the campaign in
Crete, whereas the regiment was commanded both before
and again after the campaign by Brigadier General Meindl.

22. EXPERIMENTATION WITH MILITARY GLIDERS

After the Cretan episode, experiments in the glider
transport of large numbers of troops into simulated enemy
territory were begun at the Experimental Department
(*Versuchsabteilung*) of Berlin. With promise of success,
the experiments were continued and intensified on the
airfields of Stendal and of Lager Linde near Grossborn.
In mid-1942, secret experimentation with gliders carrying
as many as 50 or more men were being conducted offi-
cially on the airfields of Stendal, Hildesheim, Halberstadt,

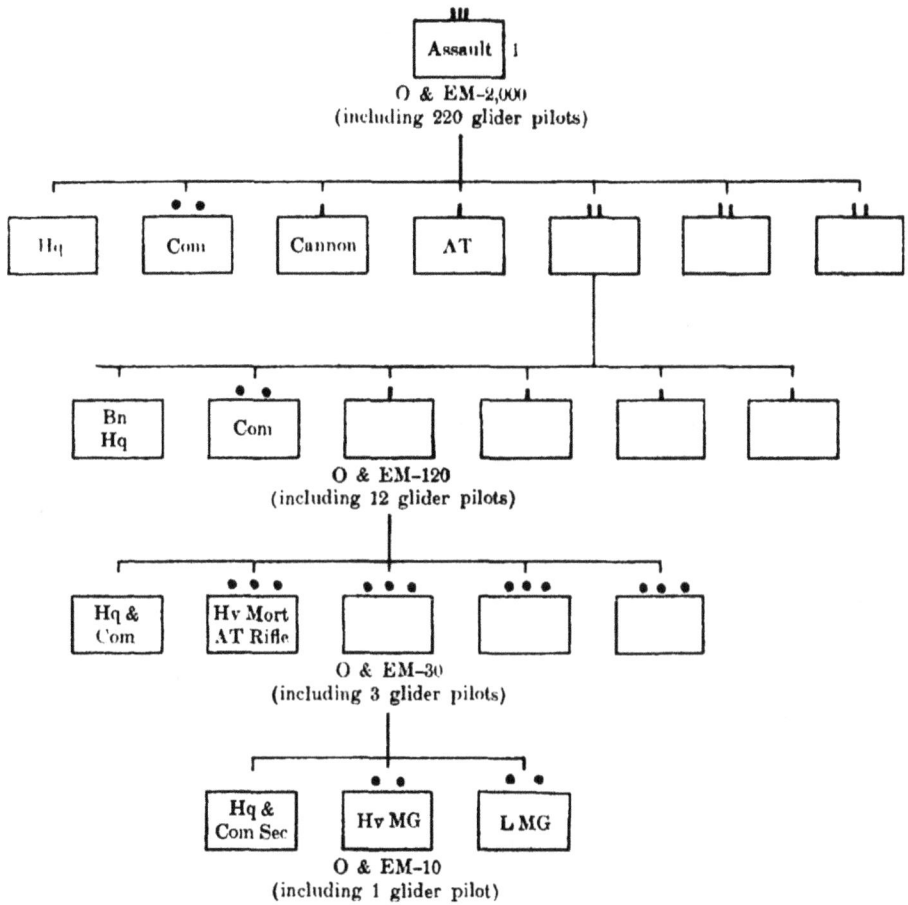

Armament for the 1st Assault Regiment:

The total armament is uncertain, but one estimate gives the following:

Light machine guns	120
Heavy machine guns	36
Heavy mortars (81-mm)	12
AT rifles	12

Figure 4.—Organization of the German 1st Assault Regiment

Hanover, and Berlin. Tests in carrying all-purpose vehicles and tanks have been frequent.

23. GLIDER-BORNE PERSONNEL

All glider pilots and glider-borne troops and the 1st Assault Regiment are members of the German Air Force, though they may initially have been in the Army. Glider pilots are generally men who have had previous civilian experience in glider flying. But comparatively excellent civilian glider experience is said to be insufficient to qualify a pilot for operating a freight-carrying model. Training on the large gliders is done in the glider unit itself. An important feature is the making of spot landings, and blind flying is also taught. At the glider training school at Braunschweig-Waggum, the course lasts 6 weeks. No reserve pilot is carried in operations with the small glider. Air-landing troops do not necessarily have to have any special training beyond instruction and practice in getting out of the glider quickly.

24. THE DFS-230 GLIDER

The glider used by the Germans in Crete was a high-wing 10-seater monoplane. It is known as the DFS–230 freight-carrying glider (*Lastensegler* or *Lastensegelflugzeug*, abbreviated *L. S.*). It has probably been in production since the spring of 1940, and in quantity production since autumn of that year. In the spring of 1942, a minimum estimate of the number on hand was 700.

a. Construction

It is believed that the fuselage is of tubular steel construction, and that the wings are made entirely of wood.

Usually the glider's wheels have been jettisoned after take-off, the glider landing on its skid.

b. Seating Arrangements

The interior arrangements are not spacious. The seats are in a single line, six facing forward and four backward. The four rear seats can be taken out to provide more space for freight. The DFS–230 is designed to carry a pilot and 9 men, with equipment. For rapid exit from the glider, each end is fitted with a door.

c. Dimensions

The approximate dimensions of the DFS–230 are given as follows: span, 72 feet; length, 36 feet.

d. Weight and Load Statistics

Various weights, according to various uses made of the glider, are as follows (in pounds):

Weight empty, including fixed equipment	1,818	1,818	1,818
Useful load	2,371	2,485	2,433
Gross weight	4,189	4,305	4,251

e. Equipment

Instruments are phosphorescent, and include air speed indicator, altimeter, rate-of-climb indicator, turn-and-bank indicator, and compass. A 24-volt storage battery is fitted in the nose to operate navigation lights, cabin lights, and a landing light, which is under the port wing. A fixed light machine gun (LMG 34) is said to be attached externally to the starboard side, and is fired by the man in No. 2 seat (sitting behind the pilot), through a slit in the fuselage, as the glider is landing. Aiming of the machine gun is not possible.

f. Towing Planes

Under combat conditions, the Ju–52 aircraft, which is ordinarily used to tow the DFS–230 glider, normally flies empty. This is because the towing plane does not fly over the objective, but releases the gliders, each of which is attached to it directly, in V-formation: glider "trains" are not used. In operations, normally one glider is towed: three Ju–52's with their gliders, fly in formation. Types such as the Me–110 or He–111 are quite suitable for use as towing aircraft. In training, and probably also for freight-carrying in rear areas, other aircraft are used for towing, including the He–45 and He–46 (training aircraft) and the Henschel–126 (army cooperation aircraft). Fighter planes have also been used to tow gliders in training. A table of tug and glider performances is given in figure 5.

g. Length of Tow-Rope

Tow-ropes are of varying length, 40, 60, 100, or 120 yards, according to the airfield space available. The glider handles better with a longer rope. Runways are ideal for the take-off, but are not essential.

h. Towing Distances

The distances for which the glider can be towed depend upon the range of the aircraft and the weather conditions. With extra fuel, a Ju–52 can tow a DFS–230 more than 1,000 miles. ,

i. Gliding Distances

The distances which the glider can cover after release from the towing plane are variable, and depend upon such factors as windspeed, altitude of release, direction of wind relative to line of flight, navigation errors, and evasive action. In the attack on Crete **gliders are thought** to have been released at no more than 2 to 5 miles from shore, and at heights of not more than 5,000 feet.

j. Table of Glider Speeds:

Towing speed _ _ _ _ _ _ _ _ _   _ 105 mph
Optimum gliding speed _ 71.4 mph
Holding-off speed _ 55 mph
Landing speed _ 35–40 mph

k. Landing Area

The DFS–230 glider requires only a small landing area. It has been noted that flaps may be used to steepen the angle of glide. If the skid is wound with barbed wire, or fitted with arresting hooks, landing in an even smaller area is practicable.

25. THE GOTHA 242 GLIDER

The Gotha 242 Glider, larger than the DFS–230, is used for troop transport in training and for freight-carrying. Six of them were captured partially destroyed at Derna. The flying characteristics are said to be such that any pilot can handle one with ease, either towed or solo. Steep turns, nevertheless, are to be avoided, and acrobatics are forbidden. Recent photographic reconnaissance has identified two powered types, experimentally equipped, respectively, with twin air-cooled radial, and twin in-line, engines.

a. Construction

The Gotha 242 is a twin-boom monoplane, with fuselage of tubular metal construction, and wings, tail boom, and tail unit made of wood. Landing is effected on three

skids or on wheels, the latter of which can be jettisoned.[1]
The central fuselage (37 feet long) is detachable, and is
also hinged at the top, forward of the trailing edge of the
wing, on which hinge the rear portion lifts upwards,
making an opening 7 feet by 6 feet for loading by means
of ramps which are carried in the aircraft.

b. Dimensions

The Gotha 242 has a span of 79 feet and a length of
52½ feet.

c. Crew and Armament

This glider carries two pilots. Control is dual, and the
first pilot's seat is fully armored to a thickness of from one-
tenth to three-tenths of an inch. Four light machine guns
are fitted, two firing forward from the nose, and two firing
aft; four more may be fitted in lateral positions.

d. Equipment

Instruments are more numerous than in the DFS–230
and include a telephone for communication with the towing aircraft, activated, with the remainder of the electrical
installation, by a 24-volt storage battery. A landing light
is fitted underneath the port wing. Two first-aid kits are
carried, and a ballast container capable of holding up to
925 pounds.[2]

e. Seating Arrangements

When fitted with seats, the Gotha 242 holds 21 fully
equipped men in addition to the 2 pilots.

---

[1] Some of these gliders are said to have retractable landing gear.
[2] Ballast is used only when the glider is empty.

f. Weight and Load Statistics

The empty weight of this glider, with fixed equipment, is 7,168 pounds. The gross weight is 12,750 pounds, leaving a useful load of 5,582 pounds. Freight storage space is 20 by 8 by 6½ feet.

g. Towing

The Gotha 242 is normally towed by one Ju–52, by means of a steel cable 80 to 300 yards long. An arrester gear may be fitted to shorten the landing run.

h. Table of Glider Speeds

Maximum towing speed	149 mph
Maximum gliding speed	180 mph
Minimum gliding speed (when landing fully loaded)	87 mph

26. OTHER TYPES OF GERMAN GLIDERS

Besides the DFS–230 and the Gotha 242, other types of gliders have been tried out by the Germans. Three less known types are mentioned to show that glider-development in Germany seems to be tending toward more capacious models.

a. The Merseburg Glider

A more or less experimental type of glider, the Merseburg is said to have a span of about 175 feet and a length of 94 feet. Its load might theoretically be over 20,000 pounds, but is probably less; one Ju–52 could not tow it, if the load were so high. Towing by two or three aircraft is, however, technically possible. The Merseburg glider, with a fuselage breadth of 9 to 10 feet, is wide enough to take the 9-ton tank, Pz. Kw. II. The num-

for every foot of height at launching, the glider can theoretically cover 16 feet measured horizontally. In the attack on Crete it is reported that gliders were released at an altitude of 5,000 feet. This altitude, under normal conditions and with the loaded DFS–230 glider, would permit a gliding range of about 8 to 10 miles. However, all estimates as to gliding ranges are very uncertain, and subject to revision.

	Take-off distance (ft)	Initial climb (ft per min)	Total range [1]	Mean speed with glider (in mph) and altitude (in ft)
Ju–52—fuel, 530 gals plus 1-ton payload. 1 Glider DFS–230			850	100/5,000
Ju–52—fuel, 530 gals:				
1 Glider DFS–230	1, 110		780	110/5,000
3 Gliders DFS–230	1, 410	750	600	100/5,000
Ju–52—fuel, 1,060 gals:				
1 Glider DFS–230	1, 320	950	1, 600	110/5,000
3 Gliders DFS–230	1, 710	660	1, 270	110/5,000
2 Ju–52—fuel, 1,060 gals each. 1 Glider Merseburg	2, 700	350	1, 000	110/
3 Ju–52—fuel, 1,060 gals each. 1 Glider Go–242	2, 610	340	990	110/5,000
1 Ju–52—fuel, 530 gals. 1 Glider Go–242	2, 160	380	468	110/5,000
Me–109—fuel, 154 gals. 1 Glider DFS–230	2, 760	900	500	140/10,000
Me–110—fuel, 280 gals. 1 Glider DFS–230	2, 310	980	520	140/10,000
Me–110—fuel (auxiliary tanks), 530 gals. 1 Glider			760	210/

[1] Total range, the plane towing the glider all the way and not returning to base. A rough formula for calculating the plane's radius of action is the following: $\frac{Range}{2} \times .80 =$ Radius of action.

Figure 5. Table of tug and glider performances (estimated)

28. THE DROPPING OF PARACHUTISTS FROM GLIDERS

It has often been reported that in training, men jump by parachute from gliders. Some observers reported that this method was used in Crete, but the reports are unconfirmed. It is certain that glider-borne troops do not normally wear parachutes (in Crete they had life jackets), and are technically not parachute troops but air-landing troops. Moreover, the DFS–230 is most unsuitable for the dropping of parachute troops.

29. SUCCESS AND WEAKNESS OF GLIDERS

The enemy was apparently satisfied with the success of the glider both in Belgium and in the Mediterranean. In Crete, however, it was found that the gliders were vulnerable if they came low near Allied troops. Their flight was very slow, and the crews could be killed before landing; hits in the forward part resulted in crashes, the pilot being killed or the reserve ammunition exploded. Where the ground was rocky, gliders were badly smashed on landing, and the crews and their equipment severely damaged. Some further disasters were due to mistakes by pilots; tow ropes snapped, owing, for instance, to the towing aircraft's making too short a turn, and gliders were released prematurely. This last mistake cost the lives of Major General Sussmann and his staff. In 1941–2, the construction of German gliders and the training of glider pilots was increased, and gliders were extensively employed for conveying material to North Africa. Their use is not restricted by any lack of air bases, for standard types of tow-planes like the Ju–52 do not require especially long runways. The latest gliders have been seen on some German airdromes which not only are small but which have no runways at all.

Section V. GERMAN AIR-BORNE TRANSPORT

30. XIth AIR-BORNE CORPS

A German air-borne corps was first heard of early in 1941. This was the XIth Air-Borne Corps (called by the British, XI Air Corps), which contained the 7th Air-Borne Division and the 1st Assault Regiment. The XIth Air-Borne Corps is divided into two main parts: an air-transport organization and an air-transported part. The connections between the two are flexible in the sense that transport for any one unit of troops may be variously provided by different parts of the transport organization. (See fig. 6.)

31. GAF AIR-BORNE TROOPS AND ARMY AIR-LANDING TROOPS

In Holland and in Crete the German Air Force parachute troops were supported by army air-landing troops. It is believed that in any considerable undertaking the XIth Air-Borne Corps would be supported by army air-landing troops. Any ground troops can be pressed into such service, but, preferably, air-landing troops are taken from among the best infantry and mountain regiments, if possible only from combat regiments. Troops may be loaded into transport planes or even into gliders without having been previously trained in emplaning and deplaning. The Germans are quite prepared to do this on a mass basis.

32. THE IMPORTANCE OF NATIONAL AIR POWER

The size and qualities of a nation's air forces very directly influence its readiness for air-borne operations. Almost every kind of aircraft may conceivably be useful to insure the success of a well-planned undertaking. Troop-carrying and glider-towing planes, absolutely es-

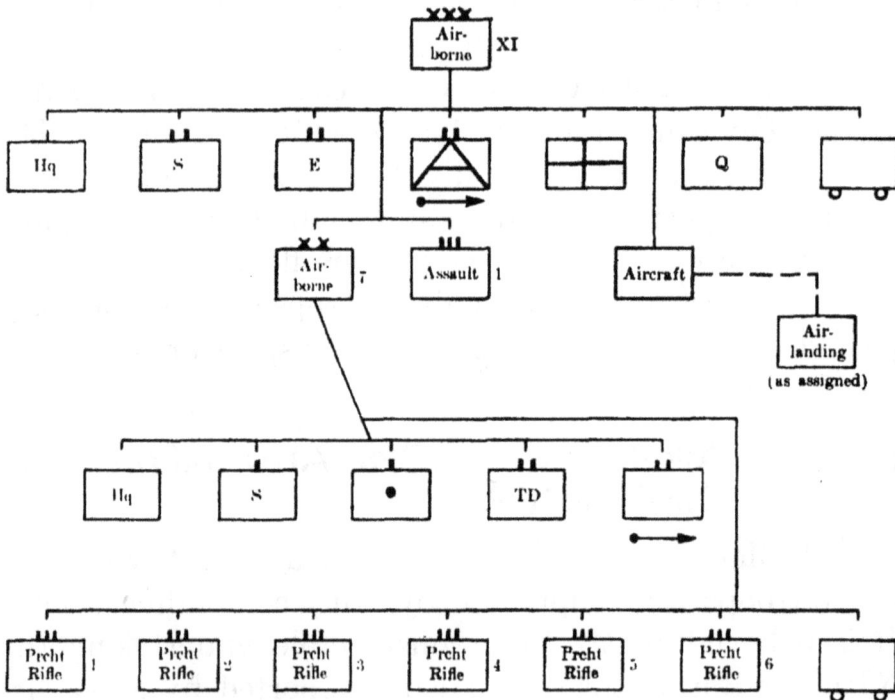

Figure 6. Organization of the German XIth Air-Borne Corps

sential for mass air-borne transport, are the types to be emphasized below.

33. THE GERMAN TRANSPORT PLANE JU-52

The all-metal Ju-52 is the backbone of German air-borne strength. So important is the Ju-52 that some observers have tended to believe that the Ju-52 was the basic factor in the makeup of the German system of air-borne units. The German Army probably adopted the Ju–52 for air transport because there were so many of this type on hand at the beginning of the war, because so many supercharged engines were available, and because so many pilots had been trained on this type. Jigs and manufacturing facilities were already set up, and, though obsolescent, the Ju–52 had most of the following characteristics, which had been set up for a suggested new plane in this category:

(1) Ability to operate in small or temporary fields with heavy loads,

(2) Cheapness of construction,

(3) Simplicity and ruggedness of construction,

(4) Simplicity in operation,

(5) Easy field maintenance,

(6) Ability to fly with one engine out of commission,

(7) Ability to withstand crash landings with reasonable safety to occupants,

(8) Ability to tow gliders at low speed.

(9) Dependability,

(10) Load-carrying capacity at sacrifice of speed.

34. THE GERMAN TRANSPORT PLANE JU–90

Another German transport type, the Ju–90, is also well adapted for the transport of troops and supplies, and especially adapted for transport of heavy and bulky articles. However, this type is so valuable that it is rarely risked in forward areas, or on airdromes that the Germans do not firmly control. In March 1942, the Germans by one estimate were not thought to have more than 40 Ju–90's.

35. THE PRINCIPAL ADVANTAGE OF THE JU–52 AND THE JU-90

The manner in which loads are to be packed and unpacked for an air-borne operation is fully as important as the weight to be carried by available aircraft. Some items, though not too heavy, may be too bulky to be loaded; again, if the 'plane is to carry bicycles or passengers, obviously it may not carry its maximum tonnage. Speed in deplaning is so essential in most air-borne operations that it is rather unusual to load a Ju–52 to anything like its weight-carrying capacity. It has been said that the outstanding advantage of the Ju–52 and the Ju–90 is that their trapdoors can be opened almost as wide as the aircraft on either the top or the bottom of the fuselage.

36. COMPARISON OF THE JU–52 WITH THE JU–90

The tabulation in figure 7 shows how the Ju–52 and the Ju–90 compare in a number of important particulars. The Ju–90 has two types of engines, either radial or liquid-cooled. Performances shown in the right-hand column are for the Ju–90 with liquid-cooled engines.

	Ju-52	Ju-90
Make	Junkers	Junkers
Description	3-engined low-wing metal monoplane	4-engined low-wing all-metal monoplane
Wing span	96 ft	115 ft
Wing area	1,190 ft	1,980 ft
Length	62 ft	85 ft
Height	15 ft	21 ft
Armament	One 7.9-mm MG, forward	One 7.9-mm MG, forward fuselage
	One 7.9-mm MG, ventral	One 7.9-mm. MG, tail
	Two 7.9-mm MG, lateral	One 13-mm MG, dorsal
Weight:	One 7.9-mm MG, forward	
Empty (including radio):		
Civilian passenger type	13,255 lbs	Empty with equipment, 36,200 lbs
Military passenger type	12,720 lbs	Normal all up weight, 51,000 lbs
Freight aircraft	12,420 lbs	Overload weight, 54,000 lbs
Normal loaded weight	20,300 lbs	Disposable load at maximum overload, 29,800 lbs
Overload weight	23,100 lbs	
Performance:		
Maximum speed	180 mph at 5,500 ft (165 at sea level	Maximum speed 218 mph at 3,500 ft
Cruising speed at 70%	180 mph (132 at sea level	Maximum speed 260 mph at 15,000 ft
		Cruising speed 230 mph
		Cruising speed at 5,000 ft 177 mph
Landing speed at normal weight	62 mph	
Ceiling	20,000 ft	Ceiling 19,000 ft

Typical loads and performances

	Ju-52			Ju-90	
Useful load	3,000 lbs	5,000 lbs	7,500 lbs	22,000 lbs	10,000 lbs
Range (mi)	1,070–830	780–600	250–190	800	2,200
Speed (mph)	110–140	120–150	120–150	230	230
Bomb capacity	Maximum 5,000 lbs			Normal 4,400 lbs	

Figure 7. Table comparing the Ju-52 and the Ju-90

37. RANGE AND LOAD OF GERMAN TRANSPORT AIRCRAFT

The estimated range and useful load of several types of German transport aircraft are shown in the following table, loads and ranges being variable:[1]

Transport Type	Cargo Weight	Maximum Range
Ju–52 (some on pontons)	3, 000 lbs	1, 070 mi
Ju–52	5, 000 lbs	780 mi
Ju–52	7, 500 lbs	250 mi
Ju–86	5, 000 lbs	930 mi
Ju–90	15, 000 lbs	1, 300 mi
FW–200	13, 700 lbs	1, 275 mi
FW–200	10, 000 lbs	770 mi

38. AIR TRANSPORT ORGANIZATION

Transport planes are generally organized in a wing (*Geschwader*) of 4 groups (*Gruppen*), each group having 4 squadrons (*Staffeln*) of 12 planes each plus a headquarters squadron, as further explained below. With each Ju–52 carrying approximately 10 men fully equipped one of these wings will transport a parachute regiment with all its equipment.

It is reported that such Z. B. V. transport units (*Zur Besonderen · Verwendung*, for special employment) were used on the Russian Front in 1942 for bringing up supplies of fuel and ammunition and, probably, delivering provisions to troops in forward areas and returning to their bases with wounded. The more active areas for air transport continue to be Northern France, Belgium, Holland, Northern Germany, and the Russian Front. There has

---

[1] Range depends partly on speed.

been also, of course, trans-Mediterranean traffic to and from Libya.

39. TRANSPORT OF A GERMAN AIR-BORNE DIVISION

It has been mentioned above that no long training period is necessary to prepare a normal German division for use in an air-infantry operation. The preparation is more a problem of organization than one of training. The German 22d Infantry Regiment was reorganized as an Air-Borne Infantry Division in 1940, and, as such, it took part in the campaign in Holland. It should be noted that this division is particularly strong in staff organization, which, of course, is desirable for supervision and to compensate for probable loss among the staff during transport by air and during early ground action. The approximate power of this division was estimated in late 1940 as follows:

Officers	241
Noncommissioned officers	1, 105
Enlisted men	5, 334
Mountain cannon, 75-mm	24
Antitank cannon, 37-mm	30
Heavy machine guns	60
Light machine guns	125
Antiaircraft guns, 20-mm	16
Light infantry cannon	3
Light grenade throwers	54
Heavy grenade throwers	36
Antitank rifles (*Panzerbüchsen*)	112
Machine pistols	375
Rifles	4, 371

Any discrepancy between heavy machine guns and antitank weapons shown in the above tabulation and those listed in an organization chart may be due to extra weapons carried in reserve. On the way to combat, troops of this division had in their packs 2 days' rations in addition to the "iron" ration. No field kitchens were carried. It was intended to use the kitchens in hotels and inns, and, after the first 3 days, to requisition food and all vehicles from the civil population, if necessary.

a. Operational Experience in Holland

A loading unit (*Ladeeinheit*) is a load of men and equipment or both together, sufficient for one Ju–52. In the operation at The Hague, the total number of loading units was not less than 866, and the number of men in the "division" transported has been calculated as 7,400. This works out at between 8 and 9 men (with proportional share of divisional equipment) per Ju–52. Of the planes transporting the divisional staff, none carried more than 9 men. Infantry traveled at 12 or even 14 men per plane; engineers at about 10 per plane; motorcycle units, with solo machines, at 6 or 7 per plane. A light infantry gun probably was accompanied by about 6 men in the same plane, while probably 2 more planes would carry the ammunition and additional personnel.

b. Operational Experience in the Conquest of Crete

For the attack on Crete, the Germans are thought to have carried fewer men and more equipment per Ju–52. The ordinary infantry battalion may have traveled at only about 10 men, with equipment, per Ju–52. The number of aircraft which the Germans used in the operation is conservatively estimated at nearly 800 bombers and fighters, 500 transport planes, and 75 gliders. In any case it is not thought that more than 650 Ju–52's were employed. To get something like 35,000 men to Crete in a period of 10 days, it is estimated that each Ju–52 must have made on the average about 6 sorties.

40. TRANSPORT OF AIR-LANDING TROOPS BY JU–52's

The following table gives the approximate number of loading units required to transport various organizations with their organizational equipment. The calculations take into account a reduction to combat strength for air transport, but composition and armament are obviously subject to further variation depending upon special circumstances:

Unit or Detachment (As prepared for air transport)	Appropriate Loading Units (1 per each Ju–52)
Inf Rifle Co	12
Inf Hv Wpns Co	21
Inf Bn Hq	3
Inf Regtl Hq and Com Det	5
Arty Btry (with 75-mm Mtn guns only)	16
Arty Bn Hq (with 75-mm Mtn guns only)	6
Arty Regtl Hq and Com Det (with 75-mm Mtn guns only)	18
AA MG Co	12
AT Co	14
Div Med Co	14
Div Sup Co	14
Inf Div Hq	12

41. TRANSPORTATION OF GERMAN PARACHUTE UNITS

German parachute units and equipment are specially adapted to fit into the Ju–52 system of transportation. In both Crete and Holland it has been demonstrated that the following loading practices are customary:

a. Transportation of a Parachute Company

One company of parachute troops is transported by one squadron (*Staffel*) of Ju–52's (12 aircraft). In the case of the parachute rifle company, every Ju–52 carries 12 men and 4 arms containers. The precise loading units for the parachute heavy weapons company are not known. Each Ju–52 takes rather more than one section, and each flight (*Kette*) of three aircraft rather less than one platoon. There seems to be no rigorous attempt to fly by platoon, though aircraft must fly in the order planned, and land their men on the right spots with the right arms containers. The real working unit is the company.

b. Light Relative Load

The weight of the load carried by each Ju–52 in a squadron lifting a parachute rifle company is about 4,000 pounds, including the plane's own crew of three men. Considerations of bulk and of speed in leaving the plane dictate this relatively light load, which allows 100 pounds of equipment per man:

15 men with clothes and equipment on person	2,400 lbs
4 arms containers	1,200 lbs
19 parachutes	450 lbs
Total load lifted by each Ju–52	4,050 lbs

c. Transportation of a Parachute Battalion

One parachute rifle battalion is transported by one group (*Gruppe*) of Ju–52's (53 aircraft). The four companies are transported by the four squadrons of the group; and the battalion headquarters with its communication section is transported by the headquarters squadron (*Stabsstaffel*) of five aircraft.

d. Transportation of a Parachute Regiment

One parachute regiment is transported by one wing (*Geschwader*) of Ju–52's (220 aircraft). The three parachute battalions are transported by three of the groups in the wing; and the "fourth battalion," or regimental headquarters with regimental troops, is transported by the fourth group.

e. Transportation of a Parachute Division

One parachute division could be carried by four wings of Ju–52's (880 aircraft). The three parachute regiments would be carried by three wings, and divisional headquarters with divisional troops (signal company, artillery battery, machine-gun battalion, and antitank battalion) by the fourth wing. But up to the spring of 1942 no division had yet been transported at a single lift.

f. Loading of Non-Divisional Units

Not much is known of the loading of non-divisional parachute units (engineer battalion, antiaircraft machine-gun battalion, and medical unit). It seems probable that each would be carried by one group of Ju-52's, in the proportion of one company to one squadron.

42. COMMUNICATIONS IN AIR-BORNE OPERATIONS

The theory of air-borne attack presupposes assault upon a hostile area under conditions wherein the only link with the higher command is through means of communication carried with the attacking troops or improvised by them. Portable radio sets constitute the basic means of establishing contact with other units, with headquarters, and with the friendly aircraft operating in the area. Because of the likelihood of heavy

casualties during the early phases of the attack, assault
units are provided with about twice the amount of radio
equipment ordinarily assigned to ground combat units of
the same size. A parachute rifle battalion appears to be
equipped with two radio subsections for battalion-to-
regiment communication, and eight very high-frequency
radio subsections for point-to-point communication on
the general company-to-company circuit.

a. Types of Radios

German air-borne attack troops, during the operations
at Crete, were equipped with several types of radios, but
two types were most extensively used. The pack "b.1,"
which was carried in three parts, weighed about 120
pounds all told. Operating on a frequency of 3,000 to
5,000 kilocycles, the "b.1" transmitter had a range of
from 10 to 15 miles. The pack "d.2" (very high frequency) weighed about 40 pounds and had a range of 7½
to 10 miles. This model operated on 33,800 to 38,000
kilocycles. Both of these sets, being very light, are well
suited for use by air-borne units.

b. Visual Communication

Ground-to-air visual communication is accomplished by
a variety of means: by flags, by colored smoke signals, and
by panels. During the Crete operations, swastika flags
were used to denote German troops. White or yellow
ground panels of cloth were used to indicate front lines.
Headquarters positions were indicated by panels in the
form of a cross, and spots where supplies were to be dropped
by two "X's", side by side. Direction of resistance
was indicated by inverted "V's" with the point in the
direction of the resistance. Various other panel designs

were similarly employed to convey prearranged messages. Green smoke signals were used to attract the attention of aircraft where supplies were wanted. Red smoke signals are also believed to have been used, to indicate enemy defended positions. In Crete some British learned the German panel calls and used them to send for reinforcements (whom they shot), for food (which they gladly ate), and for other supplies.

Section VI. ITALIAN AIR-BORNE FORCES

43. ITALIAN PARACHUTE DEVELOPMENT

In 1927 shortly after Mussolini had begun the expansion of Italian air power, 9 soldiers with their equipment made a group parachute jump over the airport of Cinisello. About that year the Italians started a course for 256 jumpers. From the first Italian standard parachute, "Aerodiscensore," was developed the "Salvatore" type that has subsequently been used in the Italian Air Forces. The dropping of supplies by parachute to the dirigible Italia stranded near the North Pole in 1928 foreshadowed successful Italian practice in both the conquest of Ethiopia and in the Spanish Civil War.

44. IMPETUS TO JUMP TRAINING

Air Marshal Balbo strongly backed the idea of parachute training. According to German sources, the Italians first used large parachute infantry units in their maneuvers at Gefara, Libya, in 1937. The main Italian training center at that time was Castel Benito airdrome near Tripoli. The training of native troops in Libya did not prove very worthwhile. A training center, at all events, was opened in metropolitan Italy at Tarquinia. Units for the latter school were raised from Italian volunteers.

45. THE SUPPLY OF TRAINED PARACHUTISTS

The year that Hitler invaded Poland, the Italians were reported to have had 2 battalions of trained para-

58

chutists in Libya with a total strength of 504 men. In April 1940 a battalion of 280 native parachutists was said to be stationed at Castel Benito; it operated in 8-man sections led by a noncommissioned or a commissioned officer, and each section was transported in modified S-81 aircraft. However, up to the spring of 1941 the Italians were still counting their parachutists in terms of hundreds instead of thousands.

46. ITALIAN TRANSPORT OF SUPPLIES BY AIRCRAFT

The Italians made considerable use of air transportation in linking up their imperial possessions, transporting food, medical supplies, serious casualties, and small detachments of special troops between Italy, Libya, the Dodecanese, and Italian East Africa. Transport aircraft dropped 43 tons of supplies to the beleaguered Italian garrison in the oasis of Giarabub during February and March 1941. Italian, as well as German, transport aircraft has continued to operate to and from the North African theater.

47. ITALIAN TRANSPORT OF LARGE TROOP UNITS BY AIR

In the Libyan maneuvers of May 1938, the Italians transported two mixed brigades by air, probably in Ca-133 and S-81 aircraft. During the Albanian campaign of April 1939, Italy relied on converted civil air liners and heavy bombers for the 50 aircraft that were used in carrying 1,100 men 90 miles into the Albanian interior in 4 or 5 hours. Unlike her main Axis partner, Italy did not, so far as known, begin hostilities in World War II with a fleet of aircraft designed specifically for transporting troops.

48. ITALIAN AIR-BORNE EXPERIENCE IN WORLD WAR II

During the fighting with the British in Italian East Africa, Ca–133 and S–79 aircraft were used to some extent for carrying troops. During the Greco-Italian campaign, the Ala Littoria (the Italian Civil Air Line) transported numerous troops to Albania. The traffic was so heavy that part had to be carried in Ju–52's loaned by the Germans. The maximum number of men that the Italian civil aircraft could have carried at any one time in 1941, had all facilities been used, is said to have been only 2,500.[1] The number and individual passenger-carrying capacity of Italian military aircraft, mostly bombers, which might have been pressed into supplemental service are as follows:

Type	Number available (early 1941)	Capacity (exclusive of crew)
S–81	48	12–15
S–79	373	12–15
S–82	15	25–30
Br–20	116	8
Cz–1107	56	15
Ca–133	23	4
Cant Z–506	57	12

[1] On June 10, 1941, Mussolini reported in a speech that in the Italian air activity against Greece from October 28, 1940, to April 27, 1941, Italian planes had flown 7,102 hours and transported to Albania 30,851 men and 3,016 tons of equipment, and that German transport planes from Italian airports had flown 13,312 hours, carrying 39,816 men and 2,923 tons of equipment.

49. FIRST COMBAT USE OF ITALIAN PARACHUTISTS

On April 30, 1941, less than a week after the Germans made their air-borne attack at the Corinth Canal, the Italians made their first combat use of parachutists during the occupation of the Island of Cephalonia, which lies off the western coast of Greece, 150 miles southeast of the heel of the Italian boot. In comparison with German attempts and achievements this action can be dismissed as insignificant.

50. GERMAN INFLUENCE UPON ITALIAN TRAINING AND TACTICS

The dearly bought lessons from the invasion of Crete and the important German technical advances are presumably well known to the Italians, who have doubtless copied freely from the Germans in their most recent training. It is said that 7 of Mussolini's men, with a Beretta machine carbine strapped to the right leg, can make a practice jump within a period of 4 seconds. Blue-colored parachutes buoying sacks containing a 3-day iron ration, a liter of water, and 400 rounds of small-arms ammunition have been known to be dropped. The signal designations on such dropped parcels have in at least one instance been noted as follows: red circle, ammunition; yellow flag, gun barrel; black circle, carriage; blue circle, wheels and trail. Such bits of information show that Italy, despite her difficulties, is actively interested in bidding for air-borne power.

51. ITALIAN PARACHUTE UNITS

In the spring of 1942, Italian parachutist headquarters was in Florence, and Tarquinia was still a large training

center.   There were probably 2 parachute regiments,
each with 2,500 men, one quartered at Civitavecchia on
the coast, 40 miles west of Rome, and the other in Viterbo
40 miles north of Rome.   During several days in the
middle of March, both are said to have rehearsed in the
neighborhood of Viterbo for a projected attack on Malta.
At least 7 battalions of Italian parachutists have been
identified.   Each battalion contained 29 officers and 297
enlisted men.   Besides 3 companies armed with a total
of 62 machine carbines and 54 light machine guns, each
battalion contained a mining platoon or company for
demolition work, a communication section with radio
and visual signaling equipment, and a medical section.
There were 203 rifles per battalion and all personnel were
armed with pistols, daggers, and hand grenades.

52. ITALIAN INTEREST IN GLIDING

There is little doubt that the Italians, with their knowl-
edge of wooden aircraft construction and their experience
with light gliders, could readily manufacture efficient
troop-carrying gliders, similar to those used by the
Germans.   Statistics given in the Italian press during
1940, and the number of gliding certificates issued to
pilots, would indicate that Italy has been glider-conscious
for some time.   The following gliders, none suitable for
carrying valuable military loads, have been mentioned:
Cantu, Grifo, Borea, Asiago, Superfrifo, Pellicano, Spar-
viero, CAT-15, CAT-20, CAT-28, CAT-BP, and AL-3.
The latter has a very shallow angle of glide and holds the
Italian endurance record.   The type for which the following details are listed is the trainer, CAT-15:

Span	35.1 ft
Length	18.3 ft
Height	6.6 ft
Wing area	158 sq ft
Empty weight	206 lbs
Wing loading	2.3 lbs per sq ft
Gliding angle	1 in 15
Rate of descent	3.3 ft per sec

53. ITALIAN AIR-LANDING UNITS

There have been unconfirmed reports that the Italians are organizing "parachute divisions," but it is more likely that they are forming mixed divisions of parachute and air-landing troops. The 126th Infantry Regiment was described in midsummer 1942 as transported by air, presumably meaning that it was specially trained for use in an air-landing operation. This regiment, along with the 125th, formed part of the "45 Spezia" Division, which had been much below strength and was doubtless intended to be reconstituted as an air-borne division of mixed parachute and air-landing troops. Its headquarters were at Pisa.

54. COMBINED EMPLOYMENT OF AIR-LANDING AND PARACHUTE TROOPS

Italian principles for the combined operations of parachute and air-landing troops make the following specifications: (1) Air-landing units should be composed of troops which have received special training. (2) This training should consist of practice in rapidly deplaning, and should be carried out jointly with parachute troops. (3) Air-landing troops require special equipment and organization. (4) The employment of air-landing units

in cooperation with parachute units will normally be
"to occupy important positions in the rear of the enemy
in order to assist the advance of friendly troops, cut off
the enemy's retreat, or prevent the flow of reinforcements
to the enemy."

Section VII. JAPANESE AIR-BORNE FORCES

55. HISTORICAL NOTE

About the time that Germany was making world headlines with her conquest, partly air-borne, of the Low Countries, the Japanese, who are notorious imitators, were starting their parachute training in earnest. Since the end of 1940, Japanese parachutists have received training from German instructors. In accordance with their recommendations, most of the training since 1941 has been conducted at Hainan Island at Sama-A (Navy) and at Kiungshon (Army). By the autumn of that year, a hundred German instructors were reported to be in Japan, Occupied China, and Formosa, mainly at Tatsuka, Nakamita, Shirahama, Shibata, Tachikawa, Kasumi-gaura, Kogo, and Hainan Island. Some training has been reported in Manchuria at Hsinking and Harbin, and also in North China near Shanghai, Wuchang, Nanking, and Hsiang Fan.

56. ORGANIZATION OF JAPANESE PARACHUTE TROOPS

The Japanese parachute battalion consists of a headquarters staff, a supply unit (which carries 15 reserve aero engines), 3 parachute companies, and flying personnel. The total strength of a battalion is about 670 officers and men. The Japanese parachute company comprises a com-

65

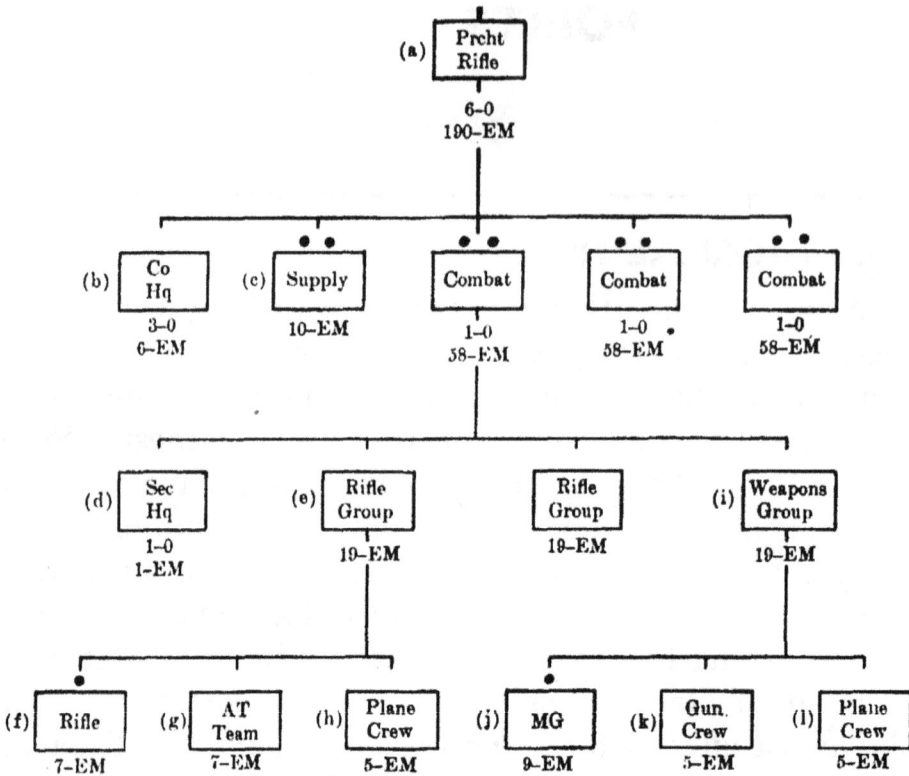

(a) Prcht Rifle — 6–0 190–EM

(b) Co Hq — 3–0 6–EM   (c) Supply — 10–EM   Combat — 1–0 58–EM   Combat — 1–0 58–EM   Combat — 1–0 58–EM

(d) Sec Hq — 1–0 1–EM   (e) Rifle Group — 19–EM   Rifle Group — 19–EM   (i) Weapons Group — 19–EM

(f) Rifle — 7–EM   (g) AT Team — 7–EM   (h) Plane Crew — 5–EM   (j) MG — 9–EM   (k) Gun. Crew — 5–EM   (l) Plane Crew — 5–EM

[(AR) = armed with automatic rifle   (P) = armed with pistol]

(a) Total company: 107 pistols, 95 automatic rifles, 18 AT rifles, 12 MG's, 3–40-mm Arisaka cannon (model 19), 19 portable radios, 1 command plane, 10 transport planes, 20 pursuit planes.

(b) Personnel and armament of company headquarters: 1 captain (CO) (P); 1 Lt (2d-in-comd) (P); 1 Lt (technical O) (P); 1 1st Sgt (P); 1 Transport Sgt (P); 4 EM (clerk, first-aid man, liaison agent, mechanic) (P).

(c) Supply section: 1 NCO (sec chief) (P); 4 NCO's (pilots) (P); 1 NCO (observer) (P); 2 EM (mechanics) (P); 2 EM (basic) (P); 1 radio set; 5 planes—1 command, 1 transport, 2 pursuit.

(d) Combat section headquarters: 1 Lt (sec CO) (P); 1 NCO (mechanic) (P).

(e) Initial ammunition for the rifle group: 32–34 hand grenades; 360–450 rds, pistol; 3,000–3,375 rds, automatic rifle; 1,500 rds, AT rifle.

(f) Rifle squad: 1 NCO (Ldr) (P); 3 EM (sharpshooters) (AT rifles); 3 EM (loaders) (AR).

(See opposite page)

Figure 8. Organization of the Japanese parachute company (July 1941)

mand group, a supply group, and 3 sections. The section is formed of 2 rifle groups, and 1 heavy weapons group. A rifle group is made up of a squad of riflemen, an anti-tank team, and an airplane crew. A heavy weapons group has 1 machine-gun section, 1 gun crew, and 1 airplane crew. The organization of the Japanese parachute company as reported several months ago is shown in figure 8.

57. SELECTION OF PERSONNEL

Trainees are selected between the ages of 20 to 25 after a strict medical examination, part of which is conducted in a room subject to controlled air pressure. Intelligence and psychological tests are also given. Many applicants are eliminated in the preliminary examinations, only the superior candidates being chosen. At the Shibata training center, it is reported that two steel globular cages about 5 feet in diameter, with a seat inside and an opening at eye-level in front of the seat, are used in training parachutists to overcome giddiness and in rejecting those who prove unsatisfactory. A trainee is strapped in the seat,

---

(g) AT team: 1 NCO (Ldr) (P); 3 EM (sharpshooters) (AT rifles); 3 EM (loaders) (AR).

(h) Plane crew of the rifle group: 3 NCO's (pilots) (P); 1 NCO (observer) (P); 1 EM (mechanic) (P); 3 planes—1 transport, 2 pursuit.

(i) Initial ammunition for the weapons group: 450 rds, pistol; 1,525 rds. AT; 5,000 rds, MG; 100 rds, cannon.

(j) MG squad: 1 NCO (Ldr) (P); 4 EM (gunners) (P); 4 EM (loaders) (AR); 2(?) 12.7 mm MG's.

(k) Gun crew: 1 NCO (Ldr) (P); 1 EM (gun pointer) (P); 1 EM (loader) (AR); 1 EM (range-finder operator) (AR); 1 EM (sharpshooter) (AR); 1 40-mm Arisaka cannon (model 19).

(l) Plane crew of the weapons group: 1 NCO (observer) (P); 3 NCO's (pilots) (P); 1 EM (mechanic) (P); 3 planes—1 transport, 2 pursuit.

and the cage then rolled about. Immediately upon stopping, the candidate must read satisfactorily certain letters and figures which are held opposite the eye-level opening in the cage.

58. OFFICER STANDARDS

All members of Japanese parachute troops receive high pay as compared to that of ordinary Japanese soldiers. They take special courses in foreign languages and map reading, and must be familiar with airplanes and engine details. All parachute troop officers are drawn from the Japanese Air Corps. They cannot be over 28 years old, with the exception of the battalion commanders, usually colonels, for whom the top allowable age is 35. In addition to meeting the same rigid requirements as the younger men, officers must have completed special courses at the Staff College.

59. THE JAPANESE TRAINING PROGRAM

Originally 6 months in duration, the Japanese parachutist training course has been intensified and shortened under German supervision. The basic training of the parachute troops in the Canton area, in March 1941, consisted of five stages. The first stage began with somersaults and the second stage with jumps from a table, the height gradually increasing to 12 feet. In the third stage, troops, jumped from platforms from 12 to 25 feet high onto sand pits. The fourth stage progressed to controlled parachute jumps from a 350-foot tower, the parachute being attached to the tower by a rope.[1] Parachutists were given about 3 months of preliminary train-

---

[1] According to one report, airplanes are used for this stage.

ing before jumps from aircraft were made. During these 3 months they attended classes in geography, topography, foreign languages, and communications, and, in addition, gained experience as passengers in different types of aircraft. The fifth stage of training consisted of "first" jumps from slow-flying aircraft at 4,000 feet. Later jumps were made at lower altitudes, and from faster aircraft. Jumpers were trained to delay opening of the parachute until 250 to 350 feet from the ground. They were told that such timing reduced the time of exposure to cold, and eliminated to some degree drift and danger of ground fire. The standard aimed at is said to be 12 men jumping in 10 seconds, as a transport covers a distance of approximately 730 yards during that time. Equipment carried by troops was increased as training advanced.

60. EQUIPMENT OF JAPANESE PARACHUTISTS

Japanese parachute troops are not only capably trained but intelligently equipped for combat employment.

a. Clothing

All ranks are provided with special clothing: fur-lined jacket and trousers, and a hood with goggles. Buff-colored crash helmets, with ear flaps and chin straps, and light canvas-webbing equipment (inside the helmet) were worn in the Netherlands East Indies operations. Japanese parachutists landed at Koepang in green uniforms.

b. Officer Accessories

Each Japanese officer carries a flashlight, a wallet containing maps, and writing material. At Palembang officers wore after landing a green khaki cap, similar to a baseball cap, with an orange star at the front, and green khaki shirts and shorts. Each of them carried a 32-caliber automatic pistol (with cleaning rod), a Leica-type camera, field glasses (calibrated on the right lens only), and a haversack containing such articles as leather gloves, cigarettes, several small liquid-filled vials, and packages of concentrated food.

c. Haversack

The noncommissioned officers and men are equipped with a haversack containing a complete change of under-clothing, an extra pair of shoes, and ordinary and emergency rations.

d. Food

The 3-day ration carried in the haversack consists of $2\frac{1}{4}$ pounds of rice, 2 tins of canned fish, 2 tins of canned meat, and 1 ounce of tea. The iron ration for parachutists is made in wafer form of ground rice and wheat, with some sesame seed. In addition, they use an extract of mussel flesh, prunes, preserved ginger, crushed bean meal, and norwi (dried seaweed containing alkali, soda, and iodine). Such rations have been tried out successfully in the climates of Malaya, the East Indies, the Philippines, China, Manchuria, and Siberia.

e. Weapons

Japanese parachute troops carry pistols and daggers or knives, used to cut the parachute shrouds upon landing. The individual sometimes wears a small radio receiving set on his belt. Other radios, machine guns, light mortars, entrenching tools, and so on, are frequently dropped separately from the men. Troops are usually equipped with submachine guns and light folding bicycles. The majority of the Japanese dropped at Koepang were armed with either submachine guns or automatic rifles.

f. Parachutes

With the Japanese export market for silk largely cut off since Pearl Harbor, it will be logical to expect the Japanese to produce an almost indefinite number of high-quality parachutes with their abundant silk. At the start of the offensive against Sumatra in early 1942, each man carried a spare parachute for use in emergency. Normally the Japanese parachute opens after 3 seconds and then checks the falling rate to 16.5 feet per second. Since the average Japanese soldier is lighter than the American, he can theoretically carry down relatively more equipment. In Japanese maneuvers, the parachute of a section leader, who jumps first, is often dyed a special color to enable other members of the section to watch for signals from him during the descent and after landing.

61. JAPANESE AIRCRAFT EMPLOYED IN AIR-BORNE TRANSPORT

A standardized national type for the transport of air-borne units, such as the Ju–52 in Germany, has not yet been revealed in enemy operations in the Orient. In some raids, the Japanese have used type TB–92 four-motored bombers. In the Palembang attack, among the craft they used were several captured Hudsons with British identifications; at Koepang, aircraft resembling Douglas types were used. Japanese parachutists are known to have been transported in command planes, such as the Kawa amphibian biplane, Model 115; in transport planes, such as the triple-engined Mitsubishi, Model 112, bomber and transport; and in various pursuit planes. It was reported a year ago that the Fukudakei factory was producing troop-carrying gliders with 25-horsepower engines to extend the range.

62. TACTICS IN THE USE OF JAPANESE PARACHUTE TROOPS

The usual first operation of Japanese invasion forces is to seize key airdromes and their environs. Bombardment of nearby air bases is a common tactic in connection with the capture of a selected airdrome; such bombing is designed to minimize air interference with landing operations. For obvious reasons, the Japanese try not to damage the runways of the airdromes which they hope eventually to use for their own invading planes and air-landing troops.

The details of the Japanese attack on Koepang are worth repeating. Transports resembling Douglas types, supported by bombers and fighters, each carried from 15 to 30 green-uniformed men, who were dropped in groups of from 6 to 8. All ground defenses were strafed. The jumpers, who appeared to make their jumps from the belly of the aircraft, were apparently carried by the slipstream along a static rail to the tail assembly, where a catch pulled the ripcord and released the jumper. The jumps, were made from 300 to 500 feet, there being no aerial opposition. In addition to white parachutes, red and blue ones were used. During the descent submachine guns were fired, and the Japanese made a great deal of noise, calling out, "You are my prisoner, Australian!" and similar taunts. Upon landing, the Japanese quickly took up ambush and sniping positions.

63. THE JAPANESE MANEUVERS OF JUNE 1941 NEAR AKITA

In the Japanese maneuvers carried out in June 1941 near Akita to test basic training and to formulate tactical doctrine, four problems were investigated: (1) the dropping of a unit of approximately two infantry platoons to carry out a demolition mission in enemy rear areas; (2) the dropping of a similar-sized unit to cover the landing of an infantry battalion transported by plane; (3) a problem like the preceding, except that the parachutists were protected by low-flying airplanes using machine guns; (4) the dropping of an infantry company to seize important terrain features in the rear of an enemy position prior to an attack by ground troops. If the reported views as to the success of the maneuvers are correct, the Japanese concluded: first, that the employment of parachute troops for demolition movements was advantageous neither from the point of view of certainty in accomplishing a mission, nor from the point of view of economy in men and equipment; second, that the use of parachute troops in the absence of support from air-landing troops or from ground troops was a doubtful procedure; third, that no necessity existed for the formation of highly trained parachute units, for the reason that with very little basic training the men and equipment of infantry units could be utilized. The final point, though a little puzzling, may reflect the alleged Japanese Army dislike for highly specialized units and preference for all-around units.

64. JAPANESE AIR-LANDING TROOPS

A corollary to the Japanese opinion just cited would surely be that ordinary troops could be used as air-landing troops with very little preliminary instruction or practice in air movement. Japan has already considerably outstripped Italy in air-borne capabilities. With her already large number of parachutists, with her aggressive air force, with her still formidable navy, and, above all, with her veteran, agile troops, Japan may be expected to try other and possibly greater air-borne operations before she is brought to her knees.

Section VIII. CONCLUSIONS: ENEMY AIR-BORNE TACTICS [1]

Although U. S. troops at Pearl Harbor and since have undergone numerous air attacks, up to autumn 1942 they have experienced no air-borne assaults. But because all of the Axis enemies, notably the arch-teacher Germany and the arch-pupil Japan, are capable of planning such assaults, it is worthwhile to consider the tactical lessons learned by the British from the classic Battle of Crete. Their conclusions have been summed up in very nearly the following words, which are changed mainly to allow for several differences in nomenclature.

65. DISTANCE FROM DEPARTURE AIRDROMES

It is remarkable that the distance from departure airdromes to the scene of operations in Crete was approximately the same as it was previously in the attack on Holland, namely about 200 miles. If the departure airdromes are too near to the objective, they may be discovered in time (the concentrations of transport planes being conspicuous), and the advantages of surprise will be forfeited, even if the force is not, as is likely to happen, shot up before it starts. On the other hand, there

---

[1] For a discussion of U. S. principles of defense against air-borne operations, see FM 7–20, pars. 220–222. Defense against air-borne troops is to be discussed in more detail in a forthcoming MIS *Special Series* bulletin on airdrome defense.

are many reasons why the distance from rear headquarters to objectives must not be very great: [2]

(1) If fighter support is to be provided, the distance must be kept within the radius of action of that type of aircraft. (2) Over longer distances, more aircraft are needed to keep up ferrying. (3) Over longer distances, decisions made at the rear take progressively longer to affect the action.

(4) Troops going into action should not be kept seated in aircraft too long.

(5) The attack itself cannot begin at dawn, unless the take-off is made by night; there is, however, everything to be said for attacking early in the day, and therefore for taking off at dawn and not spending too long on the journey. A journey of even 200 miles takes, with gliders, 2 hours (actually, it took the gliders 3 hours to get from Tanagra to Canea).

(6) In general, the operation becomes progressively more difficult for pilots over longer distances.

66. PRELIMINARY BOMBING AND MACHINE-GUNNING

The Germans are likely to subject the areas where descents by air-borne troops are intended to take place to a

[2] One must not forget that it is difficult to state definitely any particular limitation on aircraft that will hold good for an indefinite period. Overloading has been systematically practiced for years for the purpose of attaining a certain objective. Refueling from the air was regularly practiced in British transoceanic passenger demonstrations some years ago. Extra tanks added to the Me–109 made possible a 310-mile radius (620-mile range), and the immediate use of belly tanks by the Japanese raised the normal range of their fighters from approximately 800 to 1;200 miles. Recent reports have stated that U. S. parachute troops have been flown 1,500 miles to combat in North Africa.

short but intensive preliminary dive-bombing and machine-gunning attack against such objectives as antiaircraft guns, airdrome defenses, and troop positions. Accompanying fighter support will also be used where resistance by Allied fighters is anticipated. In Crete, though Allied troops had no fighter cover, casualties directly attributable to dive-bombing attacks were comparatively few when troops were dispersed and in foxholes (slit trenches), although these attacks greatly hampered movement of the defending forces by day. This bombing will cease in the areas selected for descents as soon as the airborne troops start to arrive, but is likely to be continued all around the objective. At Malemé the dust of the air bombardment hid from view the first landings, which were made by gliders.

67. PROSPECTIVE PATTERN FOR AIR-BORNE ATTACK

The air bombardment is likely to be followed by an airborne attack, which may take the following form:

a. A preliminary wave of shock troops (probably at least in part glider-borne) to achieve surprise with the task of neutralizing antiaircraft and other defenses and dislocating communications.

b. Following immediately on this, descents of parachute troops with the task of seizing a landing ground; these descents may be at several points, 15 to 20 miles apart.

c. Later, possibly by several hours, strong reinforcements of parachute troops followed or accompanied by troops in transport aircraft in those areas where the first wave has been successful. Air-landing troops, theoretically, arrive as soon as a landing ground is prepared, but in case of necessity may arrive even earlier.

68. TACTICS OF SHOCK TROOPS

Normally the shock troops will work by companies. They will be instructed to get in touch with neighboring units, probably battalions or regiments, as soon as possible. After accomplishing their initial task, they will be instructed to join up with, and take orders from the higher units which have subsequently descended. For this, radio communication will be essential. It should be noticed that glider-borne troops, though technically "air-landing" troops, operate in close conjunction with parachute troops. Having their arms with them, and not being dispersed, they are able to go into action even more quickly than parachute troops.

69. DISRUPTION OF COMMUNICATIONS

Great importance is attached to the dislocation of communications. In any undefended area handfuls of the enemy landed stealthily from the air may be expected to exert surprise and dismay out of all proportion to their numbers by destroying telephone or telegraph installations, seizing radio stations, and interfering with the ordinary channels of communication. Such a dislocation may be undertaken as a temporary diversion or other special operation, or as the preliminary to a larger air-borne attack.

70. GROUND ASSEMBLY OF AIR-BORNE TROOPS

Main bodies of parachute troops will be instructed to attack their objectives (an airdrome, town, or military position) as a coordinated unit or force. Tactics, of course, may be expected to vary, depending upon the objective. Before an attack of any importance is launched, companies will get into contact with battalions, and battalions with regiments. Companies may descend some distance apart (say half a mile to a mile and a half), but they will try so to land that they can operate as a normal infantry unit. To produce the requisite coordination, radio communication will be essential from the moment the descent is complete. The dropping zone of one main attacking body may be as much as 24 square miles; in Crete the density at which parachute troops were dropped on the first day was from 400 to 500 (about 1 battalion) per square mile.

71. VULNERABILITY OF PARACHUTISTS

The first task of parachute troops is to collect and assemble weapons and munitions dropped separately by parachute, for the men are comparatively lightly armed for the drop. (While they are getting out of their harness and collecting arms and equipment from containers, parachutists are by no means defenseless, for they have their carbines, pistols, and grenades). In Crete, however, those who dropped in areas occupied by Allied troops suffered such heavy casualties that their inclination was to hide and take no active part in proceedings for several hours. Experience showed that parachute troops were most vulnerable for the few minutes after they had landed, but if they were given time to assemble into organized bodies, they recovered their morale. The enemy has learned the lesson that it is disastrous to drop parachute troops actually among the defending troops. Also, in the future the enemy will probably make every effort to drop even heavy equipment complete and ready for action, if possible without containers.

72. THE DROPPING ZONE FOR PARACHUTISTS

Parachute troops are therefore likely to be dropped in depth around any airdromes or areas selected for attack, instead of being concentrated on the site itself.[3] After carrying out short preliminary tasks, they will then form up for coordinated attack. The use of smoke laid by aircraft in the actual dropping zone of parachute troops is considered unlikely. Parachute troops are, however, well equipped to make tactical use of smoke on the ground. They also may carry a few tear-gas bombs.

73. REINFORCEMENT OF SUCCESS

Like all German operations, an Axis air-borne attack will be based on and is particularly suited to the principle of reinforcing success. The initial plan will be only a short-term one, the later stages depending entirely on reports of initial successes being received at directing headquarters. Plans will be bold and probably not expected to succeed in all cases.

74. NECESSITY FOR EARLY REINFORCEMENT

Although it is known that in Crete the air-landing troops did not arrive in strength until the day following the

_____

[3] Parachute troops can be landed in most but not all types of country. The ideal is to have an area of unobstructed, flat, soft ground, some 1,000 by 600 yards, which constitutes a zone on which some 50 troops can be put down simultaneously every 5 minutes with comparative safety and lack of confusion. Hedges and occasional trees really constitute no obstruction, but rocky or obstructed grounds, or high winds (over 30 miles per hour) will normally cause injuries.

initial parachute attack, it is thought that the Germans would, in face of air fighter defenses, mobile reserves, and organized land defenses, be compelled to reinforce their parachute troops at the earliest moment. Command will be taken over by commanders of army troops, who will have had a large share in framing the comprehensive plan of attack.

75. LACK OF MOBILITY OF GROUNDED AIR-BORNE TROOPS

It is not clear how light tanks, if brought, would be employed. The great handicap of all air-borne troops is their lack of mobility; once they are on the ground, they are heavily laden with weapons and equipment. They might thus be quite unable, at least in the early stages, to follow up tank advances. In any case, German opinion is increasingly unfavorable to the vulnerable light tank; and for attacks on strong posts, such as concrete pillboxes, it favors the use of antitank weapons and of infantry shock troops, with explosives. The plan seems to be, rather, to bring as much motor transport as possible, especially tractors, to make possible the movement of reasonably heavy weapons, especially infantry and AT guns. After seizing the objective, by dint of surprise and shock-infantry tactics, the troops will then be equipped to meet counterattacks.

76. DETERRENT EFFECT OF DARKNESS

No air-borne operations have yet been carried out by night. A descent on a moonlit night is considered possible, but the difficulty with which detachments would be confronted in accurately determining their position is likely to cause them to defer any attack until dawn. Tactics would then be similar to those following a daylight descent; but surprise would have been forfeited. A descent on a very dark night is unlikely.

77. GROUND-TO-AIR VISUAL SIGNALLING

Direct radio communication between troops in action and supporting aircraft is less to be anticipated than ground-to-air visual signaling. Supplies (of which enough for a few days only are taken initially) will be demanded by means of flags, panels, and perhaps flares. Bogus panels and flags would effectively confuse pilots, as was successfully done in Crete. Air support will be demanded by radio only indirectly, by way of rear headquarters and the headquarters of the supporting air unit.

78. RADIO COMMUNICATION

Air-borne troops will depend more than ordinary infantry on the use of radio, at least until they have overcome any immediate opposition and have become a coordinated force. Thereafter, they will act as ordinary infantry and will not be so entirely dependent on radio communication, except for traffic with their rear headquarters. In the early stages of an operation, much depends on reports being received at rear headquarters from reconnaissance aircraft and forward units; in the later stages, the key points are the "flying radio stations" and the radio sets at headquarters of forward groups. It should be possible to jam some of this traffic with good results.

Appendix A. AN INTIMATE REPORT ON A FORMER MEMBER OF THE GERMAN 5th PARACHUTE REGIMENT

1. CIVILIAN BACKGROUND

XY was born September 27, 1922, at Merlebach (Moselle). He was brought up at Ludweiler (Saar), where his father was employed during the French occupation that followed World War I. After 3 years of primary schooling at Ludweiler he attended High School at Teltow, south of Berlin; next, the Technical University at Frankenhausen (Thuringia); and finally the Mine Specialist School at Saarbrücken. In August 1939, on the eve of World War II, he was evacuated with his parents to Thuringia. From that time on he attended the Mining School at Freiberg (Saxony). Repatriated to Saarbrücken, he resumed his studies at the Mining Specialist School of that city in August 1940.

2. MILITARY ENLISTMENT

On December 17, 1940, his recruiting classification gave the eighteen-year-old-youth the choice either of volunteering immediately for the German Air Force without labor service or of joining the infantry with labor service in April 1941.

3. INCORPORATION INTO THE 1ST PARACHUTE RE-PLACEMENT REGIMENT (STENDAL)

XY chose the Air Force and asked to serve as a para-chutist. He was ordered to report on December 18, 1940, at the 1st Parachute Replacement Regiment at Stendal (Altmark). At that time, all the parachutist replacement units and all the parachutist schools were under the command of Colonel Ramcke, who reportedly was the oldest parachutist of the army. Ramcke later distinguished himself during the campaign of Crete, after which he was promoted to General Major (Brigadier General) and decorated with the Knight's Cross. As soon as XY arrived at the 1st Parachute Replacement Regiment, he was asked whether he would like to become an officer. Several of his comrades accepted the offer and were sent immediately in the grade of cadet captain (*Fahnenjunker*) to the school at Fassberg (*Lüneburger Heide*). On declining this offer, XY was sent to the 4th Battalion of the 1st Parachute Replacement Regiment, where he remained 4 days and received the first general notions about the Army. During these 4 days also he was supposed to assimilate the whole School of the Soldier. Discipline was extremely severe.

4. TRANSFER TO THE 3d BATTALION OF THE 1st PARACHUTE REPLACEMENT REGIMENT AT HELMSTETT, THEN TO FASSBURG

From Stendal, XY was transferred to the 3d Battalion, 1st Parachute Replacement Regiment, at Helmstett. After a few days this battalion was moved to Fassburg, where the largest flying school of the German Air Force was then located and where a parachute instruction center was being developed. As soon as he arrived at Fassburg, XY was assigned to the regiment's 10th Company, which was composed of 4 platoons of 36 men each. The two first platoons had 6 heavy mortars apiece. The instruction in this company lasted until the end of January 1941, that is, about a month. It consisted of instruction in heavy weapons (heavy machine guns and heavy mortars), individual combat, and section combat.

5. STAY AT THE PARACHUTE-JUMPING SCHOOL AT WITTSTOCK

After repeated medical examinations which involved chiefly the nerves, heart, lungs, feet, and muscles, XY was sent at the beginning of February 1941 to the Parachute-Jumping School of Wittstock on the Dosse. His training at this school lasted 26 days. For the first 12 days, 2 hours per day were devoted to technical instruction in the parachute and its folding. The other hours were given over to rigorous athletic training, especially in jiu-jitsu, and in trapeze and rope work. The daily program left the students completely worn out by evening. The 13th and 14th days were devoted exclusively to practical exercises in folding the parachute. The 15th to the 26th days, inclusive, were devoted to parachute-jumping exercises.

6. PARACHUTE-JUMPING EXERCISES

The first jump was made from an altitude of 725 feet, one man jumping at a time, that is, each time the plane passed the field chosen. The second and third jumps were from an altitude of 600 feet, 6 men jumping in rapid

succession every time the plane flew over the field.   The
fifth, sixth, and seventh jumps were made from altitudes
varying from 500 to 360 feet.   On each of these jumps,
12 men, comprising a section, had to jump in rapid succession.   After the 6th jump, the students were told that
during combat, if a rapid-firing and well-adjusted AA
gun rendered it necessary, the parachutists would perhaps
be dropped from altitudes of 270 to 225 feet only; but
the men were warned that in such cases their parachutes
might not open in time fully to check the fall and avoid
a violent landing on the ground.

7. REMARKS ON THESE TRAINING JUMPS

For these jumps, the only parachutes used were the
RZ16.   The airplanes used were Ju–52's.   To be considered fit for combat with his branch, a parachutist
must have made six jumps in a training school.

8. FURTHER STAY AT THE 1ST PARACHUTE REGIMENT AT STENDAL

From February 28 to March 5, 1941, XY followed a
course of special instruction on the flame-thrower, the
machine pistol, and the combat pistol.   During these 6
days, the instruction continued almost without interrup-
tion; the students had the privilege of sleeping only 3
hours out of each 24.

9. STAY AT THE 1ST BATTALION OF THE 1ST PARA-CHUTE ASSAULT REGIMENT

On March 8, 1941, XY was assigned to the 1st Battalion
of the 1st Parachute Assault Regiment at Hildesheim
(Hanover).   The 1st Parachute Assault Regiment was

the first created (and remained the only one subsequently) of a series of parachutist assault regiments which were to contain the pick of the elite. This regiment was commanded by Brigadier General Meindl. The 1st Battalion, Hildesheim, was commanded by an officer already well known as the victor of Eben Emael and of the Albert Canal, Major Koch, who had been decorated with the *Ritterkreuz*. The 2d Battalion was at Goslar and the 3d at Halberstadt.

10. TRAINING IN THE USE OF FOREIGN WEAPONS

In this regiment, discipline was severe, training was intensive, and technical instruction was decidedly advanced. Much insistence was paid to the various French, English, Czech, and Italian weapons. During the period March 10 to April 25, 1941, the regiment made stays at the Sennelager Camp and at the Bergen Camp.

11. DEPARTURE FOR A SECRET DESTINATION

On April 26, 1941, the 1st Parachute Assault Regiment was given new uniforms and all its weapons were packed in weapon containers. On April 29, 1941, the regiment proceeded in trucks from its various barracks for a destination known only to the superior officers. XY remembers having passed through Leipzig, Dresden, Prague, Vienna, Budapest, and Bucharest to the Bulgarian frontier. Here the parachutists stopped for a few days, and they were told that the regiment would go into action at Megara in Greece on the Corinth Isthmus.

12. ACCIDENT AT THERMOPYLAE

At historic Thermopylae Pass in northern Greece, the truck on which XY was travelling overturned in the congestion and some of his comrades were killed. XY, seriously wounded, was transported in an airplane to Salonica and later to Athens. Consequently, he took no part in the Crete campaign.

13. RETURN FROM GREECE TO GERMANY

On July 10, when XY rejoined the 1st Parachute Assault Regiment at Megara, he found that the regiment had suffered a minimum of 60 percent in casualties, three-fourths of whom had been killed outright. On July 20, the regiment left Megara to return to its garrison town in Germany, where the survivors were welcomed as heroes. The men were then given new uniforms and 27-day furloughs.

14. REORGANIZATION OF THE REGIMENT

At the end of August 1941, the regiment was brought up to strength in a provisional manner by elements from the infantry, so that it had an average of only 40 percent of trained parachutists. During the whole month of September 1941, the regiment was put through a very stiff program of training, consisting of advanced infantry and engineer training. At the end of September 1941, the 2d Battalion of Goslar was broken up and divided between the 1st and 3d (garrisoned at Hildesheim and Halberstadt), which thus obtained a proportion of 60 percent of trained parachutists. It should be mentioned that the trained parachutists (those having at least six jumps in a school) received a parachutist's pay, which meant an increase of 60 marks per month.

15. EMPLOYMENT OF THE REGIMENT AGAINST THE RUSSIANS

From the month of September, it was rumored in the regiment that its parachutists were going to be employed in Russia as infantry and engineers.   As a matter of fact, from the beginning of October 1941, the battalions (not only of this regiment but of ordinary parachute regiments) left one after another for the region of Leningrad.   XY got out of this campaign because he was ordered to take a course in telegraphy which lasted 4 months.   During the month of February 1942, the remnants of the 1st and 2d Battalions of the 1st Parachute Assault Regiment returned from Russia to their garrison town of Hildersheim and Halberstadt.   They had lost about 65 to 70 percent in casualties, including many officers; among others, Major Stenzler, ex-commander of the 2d Battalion.

16. ASSIGNMENT TO THE 5TH PARACHUTE REGIMENT

XY at that time was away on a 20-day furlough. Upon arrival at his station, he learned that the 1st Parachute Assault Regiment had been broken up and that, with the remainder, the 5th Parachute Regiment was being formed.   XY was assigned to the 2d Battalion of the 5th Parachute Regiment.   The regiment was under the command of Lieutenant Colonel Koch, who had been wounded twice in the head during the Crete campaign and had been promoted for exceptional bravery before Leningrad.

17. INTENSIVE INFANTRY INSTRUCTIONS

After a month and a half of instruction at its station, especially in infantry tactics, the regiment made a stay of 1 month at the Grossborn Camp near Neustettin, where infantry instruction was continued, with emphasis on day and night foot marches of 20, 25, and even 30 miles, with complete infantry equipment.

18. DEPARTURE FOR FRANCE

On May 17, 1942, the 5th Parachute Regiment left the Grossborn Camp by rail for France, where it was to take part in the defense of the coast.   It followed the itinerary, Stettin--Berlin--Aix-la-Chapelle--Holland--Belgium--Lille--Rouen--Coutances.   The regimental staff, the 2d Battalion and the cannon and antitank companies remained garrisoned at Coutances.   The 1st Battalion went to Coutainville, the 3d Battalion to Avranches.   The latter battalion made the trip from Coutances to Avranches on foot from 0100 to 1200 on May 20, 1942.   At Avranches they were quartered at Notre Dame Institute, which was found to be occupied by only a few priests.

19. INCIDENTS IN THE DEFENSE OF THE CHANNEL COAST AGAINST ALLIED INVASION

During the night of May 20 to 21, the 3d Battalion was alerted and continued on towards the west.   But upon arrival of a counterorder toward morning, the battalion was given a 2-day rest, during which numerous reconnaissances of the coast were made for the purpose of determining what defensive fortification was to be carried out.   As soon as the newcomers reached the Channel Coast, everybody lived under fear of an Allied debarkation, the more so since a few days before the arrival of the 3d Battalion of the 5th Parachute Regiment at Avranches, an English coup-de-main had succeeded in capturing in silence, on the coast right close to the city, a German guard of the strength of a combat section; the English commander had written on the guard's register: "Guard completely overpowered; we'll be back soon." The 3d Battalion was immediately obliged to furnish numerous guard detachments. Moreover, each company had to form a reinforced alert platoon (4 sections—about 45 men). Such platoons were formed into an alert company which was kept under arms 24 hours out of 24, well supplied with ammunition and explosives. For rapid transportation, the battalion requisitioned five large buses which were kept always in readiness for the alert company. The remaining men of the battalion were used to help construct field fortifications along the coast.

Appendix B. INTELLIGENCE INFORMATION ON THE GERMAN 5th PARACHUTE REGIMENT

1. COMPOSITION OF THE REGIMENT

On account of its composition, the 5th Parachute Regiment resembles an infantry regiment in every respect: it includes—

Regimental staff,
3 identical battalions of 4 companies each,
1 infantry cannon company (13th),
1 AT Company (14th),
1 regimental engineer platoon of about 50 men.

2. THE ENGINEER PLATOON

Theoretically, the regiment should have an engineer company of the same strength and general structure as an ordinary company. This engineer company actually existed before and during the Cretan Campaign in the various parachutist regiments, and especially in the 1st Parachute Assault Regiment which gave birth to the 5th Parachute Regiment. Owing to the lack of manpower, this company was reduced to the size of a strong platoon.

3. ACTIVATION OF THE REGIMENT

The 5th Parachute Regiment was formed at the end of February or the beginning of March 1942 from the following elements:

a. About 750 men remaining from the 1st and 3d

Battalions of the 1st Parachute Assault Regiment upon arrival from Russia, beginning February 1942. The 2d Battalion had been broken up subsequent to September 1941 to complete the two other battalions before their departure for Russia.)

b. About 90 men remaining from the 14th Company of the 1st Parachute Assault Regiment when it returned from Russia at the beginning of March 1942.

c. A total of 180 men in the stations of Halberstadt, Hildesheim and Goslar-Heimstett, formed the "Rest-Kommandos" (rear party) of the 1st Parachute Regiment (during the stay of the latter in Russia).

d. The 13th Company of the 1st Parachute Assault Regiment, which had not been sent to Russia.

e. An increment of 160 men furnished by the 9th Company of the 1st Parachute Regiment of Dedelstorf.

f. About 100 men supplied by the 11th Company of the 1st Parachute Replacement Regiment.

g. About 1,400 men furnished by the 2d Battalion of the 1st Parachute Replacement Regiment at Weissewarte and the 4th Battalion of the 1st Parachute Replacement Regiment at Tangermunde.

4. REDUCTION OF EXCESS STRENGTH

In any case, when the general call took place at Grossborn during the first 10 days of May, it was found that the 5th Parachute Regiment had a total strength of 3,000 officers, NCO's, and men. This strength appears to have surpassed the actual authorized strength, since, when a verification took place in early June, there was found in the regiment an excess of 600 men, who were to be transferred before June 25 into an aviation unit stationed in the region of Bremen. (On this occasion the company commanders made a selection of their men and got rid of the worst.)

5. THE REGIMENTAL COMMANDER: LIEUTENANT COLONEL KOCH

Lieutenant Colonel Koch, a personal friend of Marshal Goering, is only 28 years old. He distinguished himself by the capture of Fort Eben Emael and by the crossing of the Albert Canal. As former commander of the 1st Battalion, 1st Parachute Assault Regiment, during the Cretan Campaign, he was twice wounded in the head by bullets. Promoted to a lieutenant-colonelcy near Leningrad, he came back from Russia on May 15, 1942, 2 days before the departure of the 5th Parachute Regiment for France.

6. DEGREE OF SPECIAL INSTRUCTION OF THE 5TH PARACHUTE REGIMENT

On June 18, 1942, the 5th Parachute Regiment was short of many trained parachutists. Only the following units contained trained parachutists exclusively: The Regimental Headquarters, the 2d Battalion, the cannon company, and the antitank company. These units had been at the Wittstock "jumping school" from April 15 to May 15, 1942, while the 5th Parachute Regiment was at Grossborn camp. The other units of the Regiment did not contain more than 20 to 25 percent of trained parachutists. About June 15, rumor had it that the 3d Battalion was to be sent to a "jumping school" functioning in the neighborhood of Paris.

7. SPECIFIC INFORMATION CONCERNING THE REGIMENT AS OF JUNE 1942:

a. The Regiment did not have its parachutes with it, these having been left at the former stations of Halberstadt, Hildesheim, and Goslar-Helmstett, with two men from each company as guards. The regiment was consequently not ready for immediate combat parachute duty.

b. The Regiment had khaki tropical uniforms, similar to the uniforms worn by English colonial troops.

c. As soon as it arrived in France, the Regiment had received the following order:

"In all telephonic conversations and in all verbal and written orders, the Company should be called Battalion, the Battalion should be called Regiment, and the Regiment should be called Division: This is all for the purpose of fooling the enemy as to our strength."

d. On the Channel coast, the 5th Regiment had enormous quantities of munitions. The 3d Battalion alone had at Avranches 65 tons of different munitions, including many mines.

e. On June 18, 1942, the equipment of the regiment in heavy weapons was far from being complete. It especially lacked heavy mortars and most of its allotment of AT rifles.

f. About June 15, 1942, the following rumor circulated in the Regiment, "The 2d Battalion is leaving for Libya immediately." By June 18, nothing had happened to confirm this rumor.

g. Since its arrival in France (on May 20, 1942) the 5th Regiment had received 60 Russian ponies which were to be trained to be dropped by parachutes from special airplanes, with opening bottom.

8. SPECIFIC INFORMATION CONCERNING THE 3D BATTALION:

a. Component companies:

9th Co (Rifle)—Capt. Baeker
10th Co (Hv Wpn)—1st Lt. Klar
11th Co (Rifle)—1st Lt. Christufek
12th Co (Hv Wpn)—1st Lt. Hohge

b. Ground transportation of the companies: In June 1942 each company had drivers assigned, one chauffeur per motorcycle and one chauffeur and one assistant chauffeur per other vehicle. Men other than trained parachutists had to ride in vehicles requisitioned on the spot, for the normal transportation available consisted of 1 Opel passenger vehicle (with AA pedestal for twin machine guns), 4 motorcycles with side-cars, and 10 trucks of such varying makes as Opel, Diesel, and Ford:

1 Trk, Co Office
1 Trk, Ord Workshop
2 Trks, Am
1 Trk, Bag (wearing apparel and equipment)
1 Trk, Bag (food for 1 day)
2 Trks, Ki (two rolling kitchens and provisions)
2 Trks, Cargo (parachutist transportation)

9. MISCELLANEOUS SUPPLEMENTARY INFORMATION:

a. The Regiment should theoretically have been equipped (but was not, up to June 1942) with 1 smoke-shell mortar platoon of 40 men, and 1 communication platoon of about 40 men having radio transmitters and receivers with a range of about 40 miles.

b. The cannon company was armed with 9 infantry cannon of 105-mm caliber.

c. The antitank company had six 37-mm AT guns and six 20-mm AA guns. (The latter were rapid-fire cannon with magazine.)

d. The battalion should theoretically be equipped (but was not, up to June 1942) with 1 communication platoon of 30 men with radio transmitters with a range of about 8 miles.

e. The company should theoretically be equipped (but was not, up to June 1942) with 2 small flame throwers with a range of about 38 yards. The several companies were equipped with radio transmitters of a type normally allotted to platoons (with a range of about 8 miles).

Appendix C. GERMAN PARACHUTES

German parachute troops use at least three types of parachutes: marked RZ1, RZ16, and 36DS28. The RZ16, which was invented and first constructed at Cologne, has been in service since the beginning of 1941, and, because it opens without shock, is fast becoming the preferred type.

Parachute equipment is divided into four main parts: the parachute proper (or canopy and rigging lines), the containing bag and pack, the harness, and the accessories.

The parachute itself consists of a silken (or substitute material) canopy made up of a certain number of panels, each panel cut in the shape of a thin isosceles triangle with the apex removed. (See fig. 9.) Each of the three types has 28 panels. Each panel has 4 gores (tapered sections), cut from a single piece of material in such manner that warp and weft are both at an angle of 45 degrees to the long axis of the panel. Panels are numbered serially in the lower corner, number 1 carrying in addition the special markings of the parachute. These are the manufacturer's stamp or trademark, which includes type, mark number, weight, date of manufacture, and identification number; the manufacturer's inspection mark, giving the date of the last factory inspection; and the Air Ministry stamp which gives the date of the Air Ministry inspection.

In a German parachute with 28 panels there are 14 rigging lines which pass through the top vent. The lines are continued down through the seams on opposite sides of the canopy and then run as free lines to the lift webs. Each line is 21 meters (69 feet) long, so that with a canopy 62 square meters (648 square feet) in area, there are some 5 to 6 meters (16 to 20 feet) of free rigging line on each side, between the periphery of the canopy and the lift webs.

When packed, the canopy and rigging lines fold inside the bag, which is fastened by means of a ring to the static line. The bag is then contained within the pack, which consists of a base (next to the man's back) and four flaps which close over the bag. A further bag, in which the whole parachute is kept during shipment, is included among the accessories, and is removed when the person enters the plane.

The harness is made of webbing and consists of a belt with a large buckle in front, two braces, two thigh straps, and a strap across the top of the chest. It is connected to the rigging lines by hemp lift webs. Each web is so made that its lower end forms an eye which fits into the appropriate "D" ring of the harness, where it is secured by a screw, the free upper ends being joined to form two eyes. To each of the four eyes so formed, seven rigging-line ends are attached.

The parachutes are automatically opened by a static cord, 6 meters (20 feet) long, fastened to the inside of the plane, which pulls the bag away from the pack, releasing the canopy. The cord then becomes detached, taking the bag with it. After a drop of some 80 feet the parachute has become completely operative and the subsequent falling speed of a man and parachute is about 16 feet per second. The shock felt by the parachutist when he reaches the ground is comparable to that transmitted by a jump without parachute of from 16 to 18 feet.

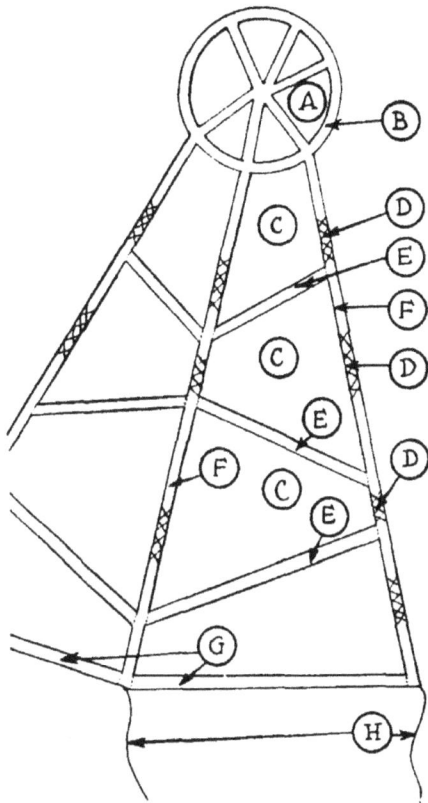

A piece of silk as it comes from the weavers to the cutting room. If the procedure shown here were followed, only the threads running vertically would be touched. In order to prevent this, the cutting is done as shown below.

By cutting the silk in this manner (lowest panel of a section), the resistance to tearing is doubled. All seams of the parachute are sewn fourfold and are said to be absolutely secure.

A. Apex in which catch lines are joined.
B. Apex seam.
C. Separate panels comprising a section.
D. Elastic joints that give elasticity to parachute.
E. Diagonal seams joining the individual panels of a radial section.
F. Radial seams that bind sections together.
G. Bottom seam that gives firmness to parachute bag and forms its lower edge.
H. Catch lines stretchable 25% when new.

Figure 9. German parachute construction

Appendix D. THE DROPPING OF GERMAN ARMS CONTAINERS

The standard German arms containers are all dropped in a more or less similar manner. The parachute is attached to one end, which has a cylindrical projection slightly smaller in diameter than that of the body of the container and is 4 inches deep. Inside this ring there are two brackets or handles for the attachment of the parachute lines. It is not known for certain what device is used for obtaining a quick opening of the parachute, but it is believed that there is some small explosive charge fitted with a fuze giving a few seconds delay. The other or lower end of the container is reinforced by radial stiffening ribs which end in a circular flange about 1½ inches deep by 15 inches in diameter. The size of the parachute is such that containers fall at an approximate speed of 26 feet per second (18 miles per hour). To take the shock of falling on hard ground at this speed, they are provided with a shock absorber screwed into or clipped to the circular flange at the lower end. This is a cylinder, 15 inches in diameter by approximately 18 inches deep, made of some light metal of the appearance of aluminum and corrugated. When the container lands, this metal cylinder is crushed and thus absorbs the impact; it can be replaced if and when the container is dropped again.

For transporting on the ground, the containers are provided with four carrying handles, two on each side. They can also be mounted on a pair of balloon-tired bogie

103

wheels and two or more can be towed one behind the other. For this purpose a trailing arm is fitted, which, when not in use, folds back into the container. The bogie wheels are apparently carried in the container itself ready for use on landing.

The containers are equipped on the inside with special devices for holding various types of equipment and supplies. A special carrier which hangs inside of the main container on straps is used for delivering small arms. All these carriers or holders are designed for quick release to facilitate recovery of arms and ammunition from the container by the parachute soldier in the shortest possible time.

The standard containers are carried inside the plane and released probably from a specially adapted bomb rack, at the same time as the parachutists themselves. The faster rate of fall of the containers insures that they arrive on the ground first.[1] In dangerous areas, however, some containers may be carried by aircraft less defenseless than the Ju–52, such as the Ju–88 or the He–111.

---

[1] It is also contended that containers are either dropped as bombs after parachutists have dropped or else one container is dropped after every third parachutist.

www.ingramcontent.com/pod-product-compliance
Lightning Source LLC
Chambersburg PA
CBHW062112090426
42741CB00016B/3397

* 9 7 8 1 7 8 2 6 6 4 7 9 6 *